THROUGH THEIR EYES

A NEW VIEW

Edited By Lynsey Evans

First published in Great Britain in 2024 by:

Young Writers
Remus House
Coltsfoot Drive
Peterborough
PE2 9BF
Telephone: 01733 890066
Website: www.youngwriters.co.uk

All Rights Reserved
Book Design by Ashley Janson
© Copyright Contributors 2024
Softback ISBN 978-1-83565-487-3
Printed and bound in the UK by BookPrintingUK
Website: www.bookprintinguk.com
YB0592G

FOREWORD

Since 1991, here at Young Writers we have celebrated the awesome power of creative writing, especially in young adults, where it can serve as a vital method of expressing strong (and sometimes difficult) emotions, a conduit to develop empathy, and a safe, non-judgemental place to explore one's own place in the world. With every poem we see the effort and thought that each pupil published in this book has put into their work and by creating this anthology we hope to encourage them further with the ultimate goal of sparking a life-long love of writing.

Through Their Eyes challenged young writers to open their minds and pen bold, powerful poems from the points-of-view of any person or concept they could imagine – from celebrities and politicians to animals and inanimate objects, or even just to give us a glimpse of the world as they experience it. The result is this fierce collection of poetry that by turns questions injustice, imagines the innermost thoughts of influential figures or simply has fun.

The nature of the topic means that contentious or controversial figures may have been chosen as the narrators, and as such some poems may contain views or thoughts that, although may represent those of the person being written about, by no means reflect the opinions or feelings of either the author or us here at Young Writers.

We encourage young writers to express themselves and address subjects that matter to them, which sometimes means writing about sensitive or difficult topics. If you have been affected by any issues raised in this book, details on where to find help can be found at *www.youngwriters.co.uk/info/other/contact-lines*

CONTENTS

Beauchamp College, Oadby

Prieet Kaur Sev (11)	1
Mila Liu (13)	2
Eric Joseph Padayatty (12)	4
Jola Isodje (12)	5
Sharanvir Kaur Sanghera (12)	6
Ayyub Rasul-Love (13)	7
Jo Andrews (11)	8
Faris Habib (11)	9
Mahana Zaid (12)	10
Cinthya Devi Vinodh Kumar (12)	11

Currie Community High School, Currie

Hoi Ching Lam	12
Shamaeilah Saad	13
Shanna Chan	14
Elissa Savidge (12)	15
Zainab Ghafoor (12)	16

Drapers' Academy, Romford

Albert Penson (11)	17
Andreja Buckovaite (11)	18
Archie Bassett (11)	19
Katie Cooksey (12)	20
Aimee Doidge (12)	22
Harry Maskell (11)	23
Alessya Birlea (12)	24
Joe Lambert (12)	25
Bobby Turner (12)	26
Riley Lamb (11)	27
Lily Grange (12)	28
Aayan Gaffar (11)	29

Keira Rumble (12)	30
Archie Best (11)	31
Mirparham Ojaghihagh (12)	32
Finn McSweeney (11)	33
Daria Scutaru (12)	34

Dundonald High School, Dundonald

Angel Uzoechina (13)	35
Emerald Dlamini (13)	36
Lauren Williams (13)	37
Shantel Chitanda (13)	38
Mithesh Mugundan (14)	39
Ellis Fairlie (14)	40
Koren Marchant (14)	41
Samantha Stapleton (14)	42
George Clark (12)	43
Jessica Stapleton (14)	44
Samira Kamoos (10)	45
Abigail Greer (14)	46

Engineering UTC Northern Lincolnshire, Scunthorpe

Georgina Healer (16)	47
Sophie Lamotte (13)	48
Evie Vanvossen (14)	49
Elwood Flanagan (14)	50
Alisha Pook (14)	51
Katherine Wilson-Dobbs (14)	52
Megan Cook (14)	53
Marcus Mendy	54
Milan Kibala (14)	55
Morgan Voorhees (14)	56
Izabelle Bates (14)	57
Natalie Barton (14)	58

Charlotte Gilleard (14)	59
Kyle Reece (14)	60
Jaydan Quibell-Airlie (13)	61
Adam Ross (13)	62
Aiden Husband (13)	63
Daniel Gilleard (13)	64
Ollie Newport (13)	65
Oliver Redhead (14)	66
Adam Charles (13)	67
Elliott Mumby (13)	68
Oliver Piotrowski (14)	69
Charlie Robinson (14)	70
Deon Millward (14)	71
Elsie Thornton (14)	72

Fakenham Academy, Fakenham

Chloe Greaves (12)	73
Sienna Kaye (11)	74
Riley Colman (13)	77
Evie Powell (11)	78
Matilda Shaw (12)	79
Finn Stroud (13)	80
Savannah Price (12)	81

Harton Academy, South Shields

Erica Cave (13)	82
Lyla Mason (13)	83
Jessica Hodgson (13)	84
Lucy Shaw (12)	85
Oliver Todd (13)	86
Millie Hall (13)	87

Inspire Education Group, Stamford

Blake Fletcher (17)	88
Brandon Jessop (17)	89
Noah Smitheringale (17)	90

Inspire Education Group, Peterborough

Shanna Larmond (17)	91

Kingsland School, Shaw

Lachlan Garside (12)	92
Lily Campbell (12)	93
Josh Bell (12)	94

Longsands Academy, St Neots

Maria Wisniewska (12)	95
Phoebe Haynes (12) & Bella Farrier	96
Georgia Jackson (13)	98
Ruby Henson (12)	99

Moor End Academy, Crosland Moor

Alex Teicans (13)	100
Iremide Nasiru (13)	101

Ossett Academy & 6th Form College, Ossett

Olivia Wright (11)	102
Amber Barclay	104
Louie Nero (17)	105

Outwood Academy Bydales, Marske-By-The-Sea

Lucy Aditi Long (11)	106

Priestnall School, Heaton Mersey

Lenni O'Donnell (11)	107
Maryanne Ratanamook (14)	108
Billy Mcasey (16)	110
Claire Latunji (13)	112
Edie Gravestock (13)	114
Amelie Murray (14)	116
Charlotte Hill (12)	118
Bethan Griffiths (14)	119
Evan Dawson-Jones (13)	120
Lola Broady (14)	121
Laibah Nasir (14)	122
Esme Maiden	123

Matthew Dansey (13)	124
Amelia Lyons (12)	125
Jude Al-Azzawi (11)	126

Rutlish School, Merton

David Annuschat (13)	127
Jerry Li (15)	128
Echo Tai (14)	129
Matthew Gardiner (12)	130
Orlando Hales (11)	131

St Thomas More Catholic Academy, Longton

Elizah Rehman (11)	132
Wiktor Surgiel (11)	134
Anyiam Victory (12)	136
Samuel Adams (11)	137
Phoebe Beasley (12)	138
Sumiya Iqbal (12)	139
Megan Carnwell (11)	140
Sochima Anaenugwu (11)	141
Zozan Sulieman (12)	142
Khadija Sonko (11)	143

Sutton High School, Sutton

Asmithaa Arvind (13)	144
Alex Cummins (14)	147
Florence Edwards	148
Ruby Griffin (13)	150
Deleena Ramful	152
Elmeirah Inchaud	153
Hannah Morley	154
Jenna Hunt (14)	155
Audrey Yiu	156

Teddington School, Teddington

Freya Nicholas (12)	157
Melanie Chan (11)	158
Seren Seah (11)	160
Evie Sweeney (13)	162
Alicia Dickens (13)	164

Ella Lau (13)	165
Sarah Evans (13)	166

The Chauncy School, Ware

Amy Hawkes (14)	167
Sophie-Ann Bilton (11)	168
Rosie Hooper (12)	171
Bea Wilding (16)	172
Ruby Dare (11)	175
Ashton Lee Read (15)	176
Isaac Man (11)	178
Alex Munt (15)	180
Malaqai Burgess (11)	182
Zac Hashmi (14)	183

Vale Of York Academy, Clifton Without

Rowan Turnbull (13)	184
Amanda Chittock (16)	185
Olivia McPherson (13)	186
Ignacio Lloyd-Moliner (12)	187
Jamie Elsworth (13)	188

Wellingborough School, Wellingborough

Romeo Barrett (11)	189
Elise Pettican (11)	190
Hattie Scott (11)	192
Scarlett Howes (12)	194
Sam James	195

THE POEMS

Let Me Be Me

Mamma told me, a hundred years ago over a hundred thousand of us roamed wild across Asia,
On the brink of extinction does that not phase you?

Today it's down to a few thousand trying to survive,
Why won't these poachers let us stay alive?
You want my teeth! You want my bones! You want my claws! Carry on like this, you won't see the print of my paws.

I've said goodbye to my fellows, Bali, Caspian and Javan,
Forever gone, this is not on!
Nowhere to hunt, you're destroying my home, leaving it barren, I'm critically endangered, I'm known as the Sumatran.

Fading stripes in the orange sunset,
Don't you understand, I'm not a threat,
I'm just an innocent cub,
Forced away from the shrub.

My family was killed in despair,
I wonder how my heart will repair.
I feel the fear creep in me,
I wish to roam around and just feel free.

Don't hold me in captivity, please agree,
Let me prowl and growl in my own territory,

Just let me be me!

Prieet Kaur Sev (11)
Beauchamp College, Oadby

A Call For Help

The land I graze on is disappearing every day,
By those metal monsters, who slowly chomp up their way,
Fellow comrades fall bravely when a shot is launched,
With a heavy heart as cold as stone can be,
Away from my home, my birthplace, I flee...

Thundering steps quake the ground above me,
Slowly wake up to find dirt and filth on my face,
Nose aching, from the overpowering stench of oil and fuel,
Why do these humans treat us with cruelty?
Away from my home, my childhood, I scamper...

Why do we exist to satisfy the humans' yearning for meat?
Should we not also have a choice to do what we desire?
How do I survive in this poor, unfriendly cell?
Where do I belong, with the humans as their prisoner?
But I knew when I finally closed my eyes, I was free...

Torn bags, squashed cans, nets made of plastic,
Crisp packets, sweet wrappers, boxes and waste,
Rain on us, causing difficult disasters,
Throttling, drowning, death and pollution,
How can life be even worse?

Panicked eyes of my sisters stare wide-eyed at me,
Gazing dimly from out behind a tree I froze,
Their captives, tall, menacing, a silhouette in the distance,

High-pitched squeaks are etched deeply in my memory,
It was a plea for help, that I cannot answer...

My wings are for flying, camouflaging, attracting mates,
Not preserved to be gazed at like priceless jewels,
People catch us with sticky, tangled nets,
Or just with their fingers, and tearing us to pieces,
But I know if I still have hope, there will be changes...

Fire, an eerie red wall of heat prowling after me,
Sand, a scorching wave that engulfs us,
Wind, a merciless whip tortures the innocent,
Water, murky, grimy, yucky and marshy,
Earth, too hard to dig through, dry and cracked.

Mila Liu (13)
Beauchamp College, Oadby

I'd Wish

I don't want to go to school, it's always the same
I don't want to be at home, it's always so lame
I don't want to play with my brother, he's annoying
I don't want to eat my lunch, it's so boring

I'd wish for some excitement
I'd wish to camp in a tent
I'd wish to have an adventure in the woods
I'd wish to watch some fireworks

Crash! Boom! Bang!

I don't want *these* fireworks, everyone's bleeding
I don't want *this* adventure, we're always running
I don't want to *live* in a tent, we're always hungry
I don't want to play *this* game, everyone's losing

Why is my school in flames?
Where is my brother?
Why can't I go back home?
I'd wish for peace.

Eric Joseph Padayatty (12)
Beauchamp College, Oadby

Wheelchair Kid

I'm that kid at the back of the classroom,
No one notices me, sometimes I think they can't see.
I'm that kid at the back of the classroom,
When they do see, they see a kid in a wheelchair,
And not the real me.

They don't see my big imagination or my different emotions,
They just make me face discrimination.
They say I'm weird and think being disabled is contagious,
Not realising that I can be courageous,
Facing operations head-on.
I'm that kid at the back of the classroom,
If only I was noticed,
I would feel I belong.

Jola Isodje (12)
Beauchamp College, Oadby

Eagle's Hunt

I spread my wings,
As in the distance, I see a moving thing.
I soar through the sky,
And I begin to do a bit more than fly,
I glide.

I pierce through the air,
Towards the prey who seems so unaware.
It nibbles on a lotus
And I, it hasn't even noticed,
Perfect.

I get in to be nearer,
My lunch becomes way more clearer.
Now it is closer,
Bunny is enough to satiate my hunger.
Lunchtime.

I soar down,
Close to where it's near the ground,
Off I bite the head,
Now, it's no more than dead.

Sharanvir Kaur Sanghera (12)
Beauchamp College, Oadby

Bullying By Friends

I have to lie
My social status can't die
The kids my age
I'm their enemy

I don't know what to do
I don't know what to say
My mind is telling me it is wrong
In the way of a song
It's not good
It's not great
But my friends need to stay
My mates need to stay

I realise what I'm doing is wrong
I realise what it is is not right
Now people give me looks of spite

My friends want to laugh
I'm the source of that
But I don't enjoy it
How can I quit?

Ayyub Rasul-Love (13)
Beauchamp College, Oadby

Medusa

When I looked at my reflection I saw a gorgon,
Tears streamed down my face like bullets,
As I felt a mixture of emotions, horrified, angry, sad,
And most importantly disgusted,
When I looked at a bee a pebble dropped in its place,
When I looked at a pig it turned into a boulder,
When I looked at a ginger cat in its place sat a brick,
One day while I was sleeping,
A man named Perseus mercilessly chopped off my head,
Thus the end of my life,
Perhaps it would be better this way.

Jo Andrews (11)
Beauchamp College, Oadby

The Forest

Oh, tropical leaves don't cease to exist
But use the dead fleas as a cover in the mist
Oh, have you ever seen trees in their perfect beauty?
If you have, you would know that their protection is
a stem and sacred duty
So please remember that fire is an enemy to fight
It's a tree assassin to be watched day and night
So as I end this poem with a flight
Know that trees are dying every night.

Faris Habib (11)
Beauchamp College, Oadby

King Bob

I am King Bob
I am not a slob
Being cool is my life and my job
I love to dance and party
I am the best of the best
I am here to impress
I am Gru's favourite
Don't try to detest
I am going to help him steal the moon
We will build a rocket
Steal the moon
And we will come back in a happy mood
We will have a party
And everyone will know
Me and Gru.

Mahana Zaid (12)
Beauchamp College, Oadby

Me And You...

Me and you, hand in hand we walk,
Underneath the moonlight's soft talk,
In the twilight's gentle sky.

Through the storms, in laughter's dance,
And fears embrace, our bond deepens in every space.

Cinthya Devi Vinodh Kumar (12)
Beauchamp College, Oadby

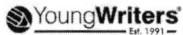

Raindrop

I rise, only to fall,
Past statues big, and humans small,
I carry scars that I can't mend,
Knowing my friendships will soon end.

Carried away, flowing in the breeze,
Past the flowers, the bees, the hills and the trees,
I rise up, like a minuscule balloon,
Almost able to reach the moon.

Alas, I halt, joining a cloud,
More and more merge, becoming a crowd,
I feel my surroundings grow closer and closer,
I know my time here will soon be over.

After a struggle, I am released,
Approaching flowers, bees, hills and trees,
I make my entrance, hitting an umbrella,
Pitter-patter, all joining in a capella.

I slide down, gliding on the surface,
Maybe landing in a forest, on a bridge or a tent!
But now, I stay in my place,
Until I vanish, not leaving a trace.

Round and round I go, like a carousel ride,
Where I go, I don't decide.

Hoi Ching Lam
Currie Community High School, Currie

The Planet

I spin constantly, round and round I have diversity,
I have air, water and food,
Anything to lift up the mood,
The scenery has no words, but when you come leaving is absurd,
That was millions of billions of years ago, now it's all a blur.

Now all that's left is stone and ash,
Just because they like a thing called cash,
They dig, they waste, they only have fake things to please,
But everyone knows I'm the only one you can see.

Fast forward to a couple of thousand years,
And what you'll see will put you in tears,
All that's left is husks and fears,
Hear me now with those weird, abnormal ears!

I spin no more as there is nothing left,
I have smoke, fires and rusty tools,
Thanks to those terrible fools,
I am nothing, again thanks to you.

Shamaeilah Saad
Currie Community High School, Currie

Tragicus Psittacus Erithacus

Hello, hello, how do you do?
Peanuts, pistachios, my food bowl is blue.
Earn a snack, say I love you,
She laughs, laughs, "I love you too."

Here, here, teach you a trick,
Spin for a peanut, tap a beat on a stick.
Clickety-clack, clickety-click,
She sang, "Clickety click!"

Pistachios, food bowl, spin and spin,
Four circles to go, a pistachio to win.
She said, "I'm going out for dinner, wait for me then."
Sad, no snack - what a waste it has been.

Morning, morning, *clickety-clack,*
Food bowl fell to the floor with a deafening crack.
She left last night and never came back.
Say I love you, earn a snack.

"I love you, clickety-clack."

Shanna Chan
Currie Community High School, Currie

The Rainbow

I appear as the sun and water connect,
I'll disappear soon, but I shan't fret,
They all look up to see my sight,
The water wavers, so does the light.

I fade a bit but grow again,
Many colours, not quite ten,
I float around, feeling the sky,
Whatever I do, I will die.

I'm flaming red, a beauty to behold,
I'm ginger orange, like hair on a doll,
I'm sunny yellow, like stripes on a bee,
I'm luscious green, the colour of leaves on a tree.

My freezing blue is an oddity at best,
My silky violet is a colour in which to dress,
All together, in rain or in snow,
A beautiful, beautiful, beautiful rainbow.

Elissa Savidge (12)
Currie Community High School, Currie

Trust

I trust you once
But never twice

You come to me
And roll the dice

You land on six
It is the end

We do not mix
So don't pretend

Planning schemes
Taking too long.

Crushed dreams
Worries are gone

You broke me
Now and forever

I'm feeling free
Light as a feather.

Zainab Ghafoor (12)
Currie Community High School, Currie

The Seasons

The seasons,
Twelve months, they share three between.
Summer, autumn,
Winter and spring.

Summer, the tinge of that hot, hot heat.
The time of play, where floral colours show.
The time of socialising, where you and your friend shall meet.
The heat shines down, it's sticky but you feel that summer glow.

Winter, the complete opposite of heat.
The harsh cold doesn't come alone.
It comes along with those bitter, bitter winds.
It's the coldest time of year.

Spring, the balance of winter and summer.
The perfect time of year.
The birds and bees and those lovely marigolds.
The floral flowers thrive in the warm, lazy heat.

Autumn, the cold is coming back.
The harsh, bitter winds.
The floral life dies.
And the creepy crawlies thrive.

Albert Penson (11)
Drapers' Academy, Romford

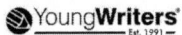

I Am The Girl

I am the girl who was playing with her friend.
I am the girl whose friend went to get the food.
I am the girl who was left alone.
I am the girl some guy went up to.

I am the girl who got dragged across the ground.
I am the girl who has lots of cuts.
I am the girl who got put in the car.
I am the girl who was crying.

I am the girl who kept crying and crying and crying.

I am the girl who got pulled out of the trunk.
I am the girl who got her hair pulled.
I am the girl who was fighting back.
I am the girl who got pushed into the basement.

I am the girl who barely got fed.
I am the girl who has a lot of bruises.
I am the girl who is almost dead.
I am the girl who is still missing after two years.

I am the girl who everyone misses.

Andreja Buckovaite (11)
Drapers' Academy, Romford

The Dream

C ausing the crowd to cheer
R unning past defenders
I want to be like you
S hooting a ball as fast as a bullet
T he crowd cheers your name out loud
I can't believe you are human
A nother signing for you and a new opportunity
N o one can defend you
O n the pitch, everyone is scared of your skills

R unning with the ball at your feet
O ther clubs want to sign you
N o one is scared of your skills
A s people cheer your name
L ike a cheetah on the pitch running fast
D ribbling past defenders with your skills
O ver one hundred thousand people cheer your name in the stadium.

Archie Bassett (11)
Drapers' Academy, Romford

Just For A Day

I wanna be a bully,
Just for a day,
To see the pain,
That won't fade away.
Are you hurt? Misunderstood?
Or just a rude child,
Who's in a mood?

I wanna be a bully,
Just for a day,
To understand why
They hurt people that way.
Are they insecure?
Or just childish and immature?

I wanna be a bully,
Just for one day.
Do they bully
To chase their woes away?
I wanna be a bully
If only for one day.

I wanna be a bully,
Just for one day,
To see why she pushes me every day.
To see why she teases me and steals my things.
I wanna see what I did so wrong.

I wanna be a bully,
Just for a day.

Katie Cooksey (12)
Drapers' Academy, Romford

The Adventurous Curious Cat

I am a cat,
I like a pat.
I sit on a mat,
I would like to have a chat.
My fur is like a hat.

I like to walk,
But people talk.
I get scared and run,
But they ruin all my fun.

I'm adventurous,
I'm curious,
I like to play,
All day, every day.

My cat life is a mystery,
It's full of history.
Imagine being human,
Just like Mr Newman.

Anyone would want to be me,
I can run a mile in three.
If you see me say, *"Bye, bye"*
I would be passing straight by.

Aimee Doidge (12)
Drapers' Academy, Romford

The Greatest Of All Time

A master-class footballer,
Strong, fast, deadly.
Scoring goals like it's nothing,
Creating history is his game.

From day one he was brilliant,
Born to be the best,
Running around like crazy,
Hungry for more.

At first, he wasn't loved,
Bottles and lasers in his face,
But, until he showed them,
His wonderful talent.

Bicycle kicks, headers, screamers and more,
He can't be stopped.
Scoring goals like it's nothing,
Creating history is his game.

Harry Maskell (11)
Drapers' Academy, Romford

Brain Vs Heart (Life Crisis)

Life is tough,
Go to a therapist,
It will sort things out.
No, it will not.
How about your friends?
They're the reason.
They're just fake,
Using me to do their things.
I don't obey anyone other than myself.
Teachers think they can make us do anything.
Make us their maids.
Brain!
What!?
Don't say that,
It's rude!
This world is messed up.
Really bad.

Alessya Birlea (12)
Drapers' Academy, Romford

Dog Life

Roses are red
Violets are blue
I can't ask for
A better dog than you

Fluffy ears and fluffy nose
You hope that it will snow
Playing under the moon as it flows
With your chilly little toes

If you are a dog
Don't eat the yellow snow
As you lie in the snow
Out pops your nose

In your winter fur
You look like you are in a herd.

Joe Lambert (12)
Drapers' Academy, Romford

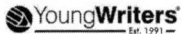

The Deadly Hawk

I'm a deadly hawk,
I hunt for my prey,
I take little mice,
And I take rats away.

And then I will take,
Them to my nest,
And eat them,
Then I take a small rest.

Then, I wake up,
And go have a drink
Whilst I watch,
The dead animals sink.

Then I'll go back to my nest,
Then finish the day,
By taking a long rest.

Bobby Turner (12)
Drapers' Academy, Romford

My Dream

J ust a dream to be you,
A rching the ball into the net,
R unning through the defenders,
R oaring the ball in the box,
O verhead kicking it,
D arting back to defend.

B ooting it up the field,
O ver their heads,
W ingers get the ball,
E nding the other team,
N othing can stop him.

Riley Lamb (11)
Drapers' Academy, Romford

The Eyes Of Boss

I'm now a dog,
Just for today,
I'm going to sleep all day,
I'm lazy, kind and playful,
I will jump about, watch TV and go for walks,
Until 3:00.

I'm now a dog,
Even for today,
I'm going to try,
To save the day.

Children, teenagers,
Adults too,
Need us dogs,
We help you!

Lily Grange (12)
Drapers' Academy, Romford

How My Life Changed When I Saw The Right Path To Allah And Islam

I was a gangster,
Threatening to kill people,
And telling people,
To give me their belongings.

I never took a second,
To think,
Would Allah be happy with what I am doing?
Then, I went to a mosque,
Starting to pray,
Hoping Allah will forgive me,
One day.
Now, here I am,
One of the biggest imam/hafiz.

Aayan Gaffar (11)
Drapers' Academy, Romford

Milo

Down I sit, bored out of my mind,
Of all the things I do,
I sleep,
Growling inside but
Outside I'm fast asleep,
Slapping my bed.

Making my dreams come true,
I wake up,
Scared,
Not knowing that
I'm safe,
Down I lie,
Falling back
To sleep...

Keira Rumble (12)
Drapers' Academy, Romford

The Killer

Throughout the night,
He struck a fright.
He left behind,
A hideous scene.

He was part demon,
He was part monster,
He was part vulture,
For his heart was cold.

His smile was sinister,
His laughter was wicked.
He was a horror,
Destined to kill.

Archie Best (11)
Drapers' Academy, Romford

My Vision Through My Bird, Blue

I'm a bird.
I fly in a herd.
I'm always heard.
I can't get hurt.
I look blue.

I don't know any words.
My vision is blurred.
Humans are absurd.
I tried to learn.
I turned around.

Mirparham Ojaghihagh (12)
Drapers' Academy, Romford

New Kid

I stand alone watching kids talk together
I stand alone watching kids walk together
I stand alone in what I feel is an isolated room
I stand alone in deep thoughts
That seem to engulf me.

I stand alone...

Finn McSweeney (11)
Drapers' Academy, Romford

If Only I Could

If only I was you,
For a day or two.
To look like you,
To do what you do.

But if only I could,
It would be good.
To walk in shows,
To try on new clothes,
And to meet designers.

Daria Scutaru (12)
Drapers' Academy, Romford

This Has To Stop

Lonely, crying, afraid, scream, terrified,
The sound of cries from a woman who had experienced racism,
Hidden like the sun on a cloudy day,
Like an ant scared for its own life,
Looking to the past,
She was deprived of a good life,
Scared and sorrowful that someone else was going to hurt her,
She was rejected, she was sent away, she was pursued,
She was beaten up,
When will it end? she thought,
She wanted to raise her voice,
But she had no choice,
Because of the laws that held her mouth shut,
Because of the consequences that would happen to her if she tried to raise her voice,
Every day felt like a nightmare,
She wasn't free to do what she wanted,
Then finally she said, "This has to stop."

Angel Uzoechina (13)
Dundonald High School, Dundonald

Queen Of The Skies

Black sky. Cold wind.
Alone without a home,
In a world that was not yours,
A short sigh escaped as you stood.
In the darkness,
Which you called the void,
Endless snow, empty and cold,
Small and weak against the tall trees,
Thoughts ran through your mind,
As quickly as you ran from home,
Step by step, further and further.
Laying on a log, resting your fragile body,
Stomach growling like an engine,
Tears drying in the wind,
Memories of warm summer sun,
Blooming flowers, laughs, tears, smiles,
A fresh start.
Don't make the same mistakes.
I've been a lot of things,
But I'll always be...
Queen of the skies above.

Emerald Dlamini (13)
Dundonald High School, Dundonald

Gone

I saw fear in my mother's eyes
Dad said not to worry
But that's all I can do
My brothers grabbed our bags
We were going to be safe

Bang!
The house shook
Soldiers shouting
Trucks pulled up
Two soldiers for every house
Terrifying
There was chaos

Suddenly, Mum wasn't with us
More soldiers shouted
More bombs shattered the scene
All around, like fireworks

Then I remembered
Granny and Grandad
I ran home
But home was gone
Replaced with fire
People bleeding
I couldn't breathe.

Lauren Williams (13)
Dundonald High School, Dundonald

Heartbroken

A girl,
Sad, heartbroken, crying.
Confused, not knowing what to do.
Standing on the rainy bare ground.
Lonely, no one by her side.

The rain filled her heart with sadness.
No umbrella.
Nowhere to hide.
A depressed, miserable girl.
Fake-smiling so as not to hurt her loved ones.

Everyone was happy around her
Like she was abandoned, forgotten about.
Her heart melting
Like ice in the sun
Standing alone in mysterious dark mist rain.

Too scared to tell anyone her story.
Like the world had come to an end.

Shantel Chitanda (13)
Dundonald High School, Dundonald

Feared Love

This is where laughter used to ring,
Through my eyes, war is a terrifying thing.
The tears running down my eyes,
We have heard enough lies.

They are filled with rage and anger,
We suffer in hunger.
They tried to kill,
We fell ill.

The streets were full of cheer,
Now they are filled with fear.
The land where we heard echoes of play,
We now see the world in shades of grey.

We hold both fear and hope,
Seeking a simple way to cope.
Through my eyes, the worlds unfold,
But amidst the war, stories go untold.

Mithesh Mugundan (14)
Dundonald High School, Dundonald

The Breakup

Lonely, heartbroken, tired.
The taste of tears filled her mouth,
The rain battered off the window like bullets.
She thought of the past with him,
Memories.
The park walks,
The long talks,
The dinner dates,
She always imagined him in her future,
Showering her with chocolate, flowers and teddies.
Why did he need more than me?
The mascara ran down her cheeks, it was a blur,
As she hugged the teddy he got her.
It still smells like him.
She misses him.

Ellis Fairlie (14)
Dundonald High School, Dundonald

Through Their Eyes

I'm a lonely, scared child at war.
I'm trying to run away from bombs and gunshots,
I can't see anything because of all the smoke,
All I can hear are loud bangs,
Paired with all the thunder and lightning,
It is as foggy as a cloud.
I think of all the good times I had with my friends back at home,
Wishing I was still there,
It feels like I've been here for years,
But it's only been two weeks.
I am scared, trying to scurry through the smoke.

Koren Marchant (14)
Dundonald High School, Dundonald

Through Their Eyes

Heartbroken, scared, crying.
The taste of the smoke-filled air,
The rain crashed to the ground,
With the sound of gunshots in the distance.
I think to myself, *will my life be normal again?*
The feeling of my family not coming back again scares me.
The lifelong fear, trauma and sadness,
Always creeping up on me,
It's scary to think what could happen,
My face dampened with my tears.

Samantha Stapleton (14)
Dundonald High School, Dundonald

Just Say No

Bewildered
A young man frightened
A whole town scared
But just one word
No

Sometimes all you have to say is no

The USSR and the USA
Two presidents said, "No"
Everyone lived

The right answer isn't always yes
You have the right to stand up for yourself
You don't actually have to say yes
You can say no.

George Clark (12)
Dundonald High School, Dundonald

Through Their Eyes

Heartbreaking, traumatic, crying.
I see the fear in my mother's eyes,
The rain pounding on my window
Like a bullet hitting the wall.
I think back to my fun-filled past,
Before my fun and safe life was snatched away from me.
New fears, new life, new house.
When will life be normal again?
I feel so alone
I call out for my father
There is no reply.

Jessica Stapleton (14)
Dundonald High School, Dundonald

The Dream

Why do you give up on your dreams?
Do you fail?
Or now you can't wait,
For it to happen
Don't let despair secretly control you,
This is your dream,
Which no one else will fulfil,
No matter how you fail,
And no matter how hard you face,
It is always waiting for you to achieve.

Samira Kamoos (10)
Dundonald High School, Dundonald

Heroes

Brave, courageous and determined
Heroes
Fictional and non-fictional
Fearless and heroic
Daring and brave
But are we sure we should focus on Spider-Man, Superman and Supergirl?
Are they the greatest?
Rosa Parks, Martin Luther King Jr.
All fighting for one cause
Freedom.

Abigail Greer (14)
Dundonald High School, Dundonald

Haunting My Heart

In the labyrinth of his arms, I find solace,
A paradoxical haven, both tender and callous.
A masquerade of love, though tainted and bruised,
I still cling to these fragments, willingly abused.

In the shadows I embrace, a twisted dance unfolds,
A silent symphony of pain, intricately composed,
I am captive to a love veiled in dark illusion,
Adoration weaved through threads of confusion.

His touch is a tempest, igniting forbidden fires,
Yet in the storm, my heart strangely desires,
Whispers of affection, masked in cruel words,
A paradox of passion, where such desire hurts.

Beneath the surface of my heart silent surrender,
Lies a longing for love that is pure and is tender.
His transgressions, wounds that cut deep,
Yet a whispered plea for mercy, my soul does keep.

In this chapter of pain and with my yearning heart,
I entertain forgiveness, though torn apart,
I take hesitant steps toward an illusion of grace,
A yearning for his redemption in this haunting space.

Georgina Healer (16)
Engineering UTC Northern Lincolnshire, Scunthorpe

Insomnia

My head hit the pillow at quarter past nine,
With my fluffy socks on and my blanket pulled up to my neck,
Laying next to a teddy that says 'Be Mine',
Accompanied by the crack of stairs and the creak of the deck.

I lay with my eyes wide open at near midnight,
Watching the judgemental blinking of the clock shine bright,
Whilst I started to sweat and thoughts raced.

Time flashed to half past three,
My eyes make squelching sounds when I blink,
When would dear sleep come to me?
The wind chimes outside, swaying in the wind, made a clink.

Time runs from me as I drift away,
Circles darken and the heart slows,
In four hours I am going to have to pay,
In the morning I am going to have to join the lows.

Sophie Lamotte (13)
Engineering UTC Northern Lincolnshire, Scunthorpe

I Am Right Here

My mother weeps about the daughter she lost,
How she misses how she would play with her dolls.
How she will not believe she is gone,
But I am right here.

She still weeps for her daughter,
The one she lost.
The kid that loved mud and bugs,
But I am right here.

I may cut off my hair and hide my chest,
I may attend parades and protest instead.
But I am still the kid who loves mud and bugs,
I am right here.

Even then, she still calls for her daughter,
The child that she loves,
But I can still hope she can see,
Her son is right here.

Evie Vanvossen (14)
Engineering UTC Northern Lincolnshire, Scunthorpe

Age

1. The age we are born
2. When we begin to learn
3. Our first steps
4. We can speak and understand
5. Our first school
6. Real education starts
7. We begin to believe we're smart (we aren't)
8. First hardships and big mistakes
9. Some people are really tall now
10. We're nearly there
11. At secondary school
12. Life's changing, we're growing
13. Starting to say stuff we're not meant to
14. Having to hide half of ourselves that only our friends know
15. I don't know what will happen but I'm sure it's good.

Elwood Flanagan (14)
Engineering UTC Northern Lincolnshire, Scunthorpe

Believe In Careers - Believe In Yourself

Open up,
Re-think the world,
Take your career into your own hands.

In the career you are in,
Does it not make you happy but brings in money?
I, the head chef, think you should be passionate,
And choose a career you will love.

Get out of your comfort zone,
Expand your social networking,
I have multiple careers and love each one.

Even if it is low-paying,
If you enjoy it, it is worthwhile,
Get a career you love, grab it and never let go.

Believe in yourself,
Believe in your career!

Alisha Pook (14)
Engineering UTC Northern Lincolnshire, Scunthorpe

Gone Fishing

Dedicated to Collin Dunderdale who died too early.

Me and Col went down to the creek
He told me, *"Stop jumping about!"*
I cried, *"We have to play hide-and-seek"*
But he just told me to stop scaring the trout

In a huff, I left, stomping around
Telling my dad, *"He's at the creek"*
I showed him the pretty rock I found
Still upset I never got to play hide-and-seek

Now I'd kill to go fishing
Now Uncle Col is gone
Now all I can do is miss him
After all, he's just gone fishing.

Katherine Wilson-Dobbs (14)
Engineering UTC Northern Lincolnshire, Scunthorpe

Windy Summers

The sun rose as I ran down the path,
My hair danced backwards and forwards,
The wind was my friend and it made me laugh,
The sun started to set so I scurried home,
My mother read me stories about fairies and gnomes.

The sun rose and it was summer once again,
I walked down the path slowly and the wind tangled my hair,
It was no longer fun to hang out in its lair,
Before the sun started to set, I trudged home,
I was too old for the wind's games,
Would I ever come to enjoy it again?

Megan Cook (14)
Engineering UTC Northern Lincolnshire, Scunthorpe

Family Love

Family love is everywhere,
The love is in the air,
Don't be scared it's not fear,
Don't run, don't hide, they are always near,
They protect you,
Make you feel safe,
When you lie upset in your darkest days,
They will always be around you,
They will protect you in the bed that you lie,
They will never disappear,
To console you,
And get rid of your fear,
So don't be scared,
They love you,
So with family, love is everywhere.

Marcus Mendy
Engineering UTC Northern Lincolnshire, Scunthorpe

Snooty Steppes

It was the first safe zone
Closing stage, there were four
Enemy combatants closing in
On my henchmen stood
All of the others were gone
The storm was closing
Onto the big house
Me and my henchmen were taking storm damage
Two enemy players were closing in slowly
Getting rid of the henchmen
Slowly making progress to me
One player took off my first shield and took a quarter of my HP
Before I did the dance
To fully regenerate the shield.

Milan Kibala (14)
Engineering UTC Northern Lincolnshire, Scunthorpe

Romeo's Rose

Love, love is all we need,
No one around,
And no one else to feed.

We are only each others,
Heavenly and destined,
Far away from our mothers.

You know we're meant to be,
Settled and cosy,
Sailing away and free.

Remember when you sent that letter?
I blushed bright red,
You said things would get better.

For you, I'd be so strong,
Although you won't let me,
I now presume that you are wrong.

Morgan Voorhees (14)
Engineering UTC Northern Lincolnshire, Scunthorpe

Check In

Posting and posting,
It just doesn't end,
Calls and calls,
And going out with your friends,
The strain and strain,
Of the emotions inside,
Not feeling good enough,
And wanting to hide,
This can all be hidden by a smile,
But people are struggling and,
Can't seem to cope,
A lot of people considering a rope,
There is hope,
If you check in on your friend,
You may stop something terrible,
You couldn't comprehend.

Izabelle Bates (14)
Engineering UTC Northern Lincolnshire, Scunthorpe

Unknown Creature Of The Forest

Hidden behind the dark trees
Under the foggy mist
Lies the underground lair
Of the mysterious creature

With razors for teeth
And knives for claws
The beast is dangerous
Yet so friendly

As it soars across the sky
It breathes out fire
That can set anything ablaze

I know what you're thinking
But it isn't a dragon
The features don't describe it
As of now, the creature is unknown
Who knows?

Natalie Barton (14)
Engineering UTC Northern Lincolnshire, Scunthorpe

Depression

Once a joyful girl,
Now trapped in a cage
She calls her bed.
Scared to leave,
But okay to stay.
Nobody to help her
Escape this pit.
A pit that's deep and dark,
With no connection to the world.
Only a small screen,
Shining its blue light,
Onto her flooded face,
That constantly shows her,
What she wishes to be.
That once joyful girl
Won't be back.
The darkness has finally
Engulfed her weakness.

Charlotte Gilleard (14)
Engineering UTC Northern Lincolnshire, Scunthorpe

Social Media - Good Or Bad?

Some love it, some hate it,
Helps people connect,
While people go away,
Helps people reflect.

People love it,
They don't put it down,
For parents, they frown,
For younger people, it's their crown.

People hate,
It isn't great.
People delete it because of their mate.

People cry,
They think they're sly.
People debate
On people facing hate.

Kyle Reece (14)
Engineering UTC Northern Lincolnshire, Scunthorpe

Toxic Love

You stabbed me in the back then wondered why I was in so much pain,
I was suffering, all because of you
There may have been a few happy and fun times
But not enough to fill the haunting times.
I may seem happy but on the inside you broke me,
I was suffering just so you could take first place on the podium.
My heart was broken,
You set me on fire to keep yourself warm.
My insides were burnt.

Jaydan Quibell-Airlie (13)
Engineering UTC Northern Lincolnshire, Scunthorpe

Illusion

It's all an illusion
It's about going outside with anxiety
Worried about people judging you
It's about whether you're ugly or not
It's all an illusion

It's going out with not enough named clothes and being called poor
Or going out with too many clothes and getting called too chavvy
It's the fact you can never be good enough
It's all an illusion.

Adam Ross (13)
Engineering UTC Northern Lincolnshire, Scunthorpe

The Game

The game started
The other players getting into position
One by one they dashed
The player slashed
Four enemies left in the game
The bomb started ticking
The timer was on
There were ten seconds until the bomb exploded
The player started defusing the bomb on a computer
More gunshots in the distance
There was one enemy left
Then the bomb was defused
Game over.

Aiden Husband (13)
Engineering UTC Northern Lincolnshire, Scunthorpe

Dog Daycare

Working at a dog daycare is amazing,
You get to work with dogs every day, which I love,
You get to meet new dogs every day,
You get to cuddle, play and mess with each dog every day,
But I have to clean up their poo,
I have to get slobber all over me,
I have to make sure the dogs don't run away,
But I have no regrets,
And I don't want to ever leave this place.

Daniel Gilleard (13)
Engineering UTC Northern Lincolnshire, Scunthorpe

Football Poem

Last game of the season
Winning this cup is our reason
The whistle blows, and all the players go
Chasing after the ball
Some players fall
Some of them score
The whistle goes
The players go into the changing room
The manager shouting and screaming
The players are dreaming
They go out for the second half
The whistle goes, and the players go.

Ollie Newport (13)
Engineering UTC Northern Lincolnshire, Scunthorpe

Trains

Stuck on track,
And going fast,
Sat in seats,
And not on our feet,
Trains have always been a good way of travel.

With a sister or a brother,
Or with your father or your mother.
Trains have always been a good way of travel.

Unbeaten speed,
Even while on your feet,
Trains have always been the best way of travel.

Oliver Redhead (14)
Engineering UTC Northern Lincolnshire, Scunthorpe

Prisoner

I stared through the bars
And lived in dust
Wishing I could see the stars
And the night-time dusk

My pillow was rough
And heart gone cold
As I have not seen enough
Through these bars I have been told

My eyes gone grey
And my feet gone bare
From the room where I stay
Lying in despair.

Adam Charles (13)
Engineering UTC Northern Lincolnshire, Scunthorpe

Malala

She was shot in the head,
Wondering why she was not dead,
Her eyes suddenly filled with red.

This is the day she would've dread.
Her heart raced as her fingers traced the wound.

But oh so soon, she seemed to regain
her senses,
She then turned her back
to make the right path.

Elliott Mumby (13)
Engineering UTC Northern Lincolnshire, Scunthorpe

Preparing For Fishing

Preparing for fishing,
First time this year,
Fixing the tacklebox,
People shouting,
Come fishing with me please, please?
Rather be on my own in peace!

Oliver Piotrowski (14)
Engineering UTC Northern Lincolnshire, Scunthorpe

Senna

A tragic end,
To an unstoppable driver,
Never failed once,
Best of his time,
And to ever live,
A career cut short,
Few years too soon.

Charlie Robinson (14)
Engineering UTC Northern Lincolnshire, Scunthorpe

The Monarchy

A haiku

The kings of the world
The power of the richest
Always powerful?

Deon Millward (14)
Engineering UTC Northern Lincolnshire, Scunthorpe

Love Sickness

A haiku

Longing fills my heart,
Echoes of your laughter ring,
Lost in love's embrace.

Elsie Thornton (14)
Engineering UTC Northern Lincolnshire, Scunthorpe

Autumn

Autumn is now here.
Summer is now over.
We are almost finished with the year,
The air is now getting colder.

Leaves fall from the trees.
Red, orange, gold and brown.
We all feel that cold autumn breeze.
Young kids jumping up and down,
Halloween is almost here!

Walking through the park,
Watching young kids, memories come flowing back.
Soon the sky will be dark.
Sky turning grey and black.

A leaf swiftly drops on a young woman's hat.
Autumn cold air.
Picking up her warm latte.
Reaching her home wondering where,
Where had summer gone?

Before blinking once more,
Winter was right around the corner.
Wow, autumn had gone quickly.
Where had it gone?

Chloe Greaves (12)
Fakenham Academy, Fakenham

The Girl And The Bird

Golden and amber, so crispy and thin,
Spiralling downwards, twist, turn and spin.
The leaves all rustled as they fell down
While all three girls walked through the town.
Some of the leaves still hung very high,
The engines roared as the traffic went by.
The girls were happy, cheerful with joy,
One girl with a smirk began her ploy.
Scathing remarks tumbled out of her lips,
With a flick of her hair and a wiggle of hips.
The girl called Jo let out a tear,
She walked off alone, no friend near.
It suddenly felt like the world had turned
And all her feelings had been burned.
She heard the echo of the sniggers behind,
It made her upset that they couldn't be kind.
She ran through an alley, cracked walls and bricks,
She was so over all of their nasty tricks.
The girls acted nice, very sweet, very kind
Then suddenly messed with her confused mind.
The trees were lifeless, no leaves, just bare,
She weeped, she sobbed, she had no one to care.
The glistening lake and the bright, bold sun
Enticed Jo so she began to run.
The willow tree's vines were all drooping down
As she wandered towards it, away from the town.

The other two girls were no longer in sight,
The sky shone blue and the clouds glowed white.
The floor was golden, amber and brown
From all the leaves that had fallen down.
Jo sat down on the colourful ground,
Uncomfortable with not hearing a sound.
She sat there wiping each watering eye
Just as a bird came fluttering by.
The bird had feathers a stunning sky-blue
That flapped and fluttered when the bright bird flew.
Some of the feathers were a hot crimson-red,
A vibrant grass-green like the ones on its head.
A few of the feathers were a fresh snow-white,
Others were yellow which shimmered in light.
Jo saw the bird, her eyes opened wide,
The tears on her face had suddenly dried.
The bird settled on her and nuzzled her neck,
And then on her cheek she felt a soft peck.
The trees were now filled with all different shades.
Jo and the bird fit like buckets and spades.
They went together like ketchup and chips,
The bird making Jo just forget all the blips.
Her smile was wide, her smile was true,
Her new friend the bird was special she knew.
She heard all the traffic, the loud engines roar,
The people, the vehicles, the chatter and more.

Golden and amber, so crispy and thin,
Spiralling downwards, twist, turn and spin.
The leaves all rustled as they fell down
While the girl and bird went back through the town.

Sienna Kaye (11)
Fakenham Academy, Fakenham

Prisoner Of Love And Hate

You nasty evil wizard, you've trapped me for long enough,
I don't wish to be in hell any longer, set me free.

You don't even love me, so set me free I plead,
I am a prisoner of love and hate,
I guess I'm going to be a puppet forever unless I fight back,
But you will have already drained the life out of me.

So set me free I plead, or soon I will die from suffering,
I may no longer breathe,
So do me a favour and set me free.

All you do is sit in front of the TV and push me about all day,
But no longer shall I suffer.

Riley Colman (13)
Fakenham Academy, Fakenham

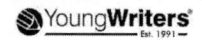

The War

Hear the trigger
Bigger and bigger
High in the sky, in the bombers
Where the ground is dry.

The war carries on
Like the beat of a drum,
Fighting and shouting.
People are counting
The loss of their troops.

An hour has gone since the war started,
Will it ever end? thought I,
Or is it a big lie?

The month is done
And so is the war.
We can finally go home to families
And love once more.
Feel the happiness,
Bigger and bigger
And the war is done, forever and ever!

Evie Powell (11)
Fakenham Academy, Fakenham

Seasons

The cold breeze cuts through the skin
The bells jingle
The snow falls

The snow begins to melt
The decorations are away
The flowers start to bloom

The sun is hot
The ice is cold
The children play outside

The leaves turn crisp
The flowers die
The cycle starts again.

Matilda Shaw (12)
Fakenham Academy, Fakenham

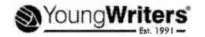

A World Of Wonders

I step out on the morning dew,
And see the world bright and new,
I spread my wings, fly I do,
A streak in the air among the blue,
I cool down,
And what do I see?
Desert sands, a lonely tree,
A forest of green,
A tidal sea,
A world of wonders,
Waiting for me.

Finn Stroud (13)
Fakenham Academy, Fakenham

Vegan

I see pain in their eyes,
May move towards her demise.
I seek the shelter for all,
But the villainous do not see eye to eye.
They slaughter and slice the poor,
Just to eat them all the more!

Savannah Price (12)
Fakenham Academy, Fakenham

I Am A Lake

Tip-tap
The rainfall comes down
And again, I am full, I am cold
Rain, day after day, always here
All of a sudden, no rain

Trees start to blossom
More green seems to appear
I get warmer, I am still
A nice warm breeze fills the air

I am perfect again, warm
The sun beams down on me
Days get longer, the more complete I am
This is always my favourite part of the cycle

But now here we go again
The sun becomes dull, less effective
Leaving me without my high of warmth
My poor trees looking more lonely as the days go on
All of a sudden, the dread is back

The rain came and left, leaving me cold
But to no surprise, the frost came next
It leaves me empty, yet full
It leaves me cold, yet frozen still
All of a sudden, I melt, now, I repeat.

Erica Cave (13)
Harton Academy, South Shields

The Sunrise

Looking out my window to watch the sunrise,
Then it went orange to my surprise,
Well done Nana, you're shining bright,
You're the biggest shining light.
I was so lucky to have you in my life,
For an eternal sleep I will never forgive.
You were my best friend,
Why did our journey have to come to an end?

I would often come to yours
Talking about my day and you talking about yours,
But yours was the same as you couldn't walk,
But you never failed me to have a talk.
Instead of smiling and hearing good news
I cried and cried over your bad news.
I'm happy that you're at peace,
While having an eternal sleep,
That I will never forgive.
You were my best friend,
Why did our journey have to come to an end?

Lyla Mason (13)
Harton Academy, South Shields

Just A Game

Let the fire of Hell reign in his head,
Let the devils fly until he's dead,
And may his skeleton haunt his soul,
May his body burn with the coal,
Let war continue in his name,
Let the Devil prevent him of love the same.

Some may say I'm broken-hearted,
But his filthy games have been outsmarted.
I'm not a puppet nor a game,
I'll never let another man treat me the same,
Even though I participated,
I'll never again be manipulated!

So let him lie in the fires below
And never have fires put out by snow,
As he cheated in December,
Which is something I'll always remember!

Jessica Hodgson (13)
Harton Academy, South Shields

Is It Just Me?

You go,
I'm alone,
Can't cope,
I mope,
You're free
From me,
Are you happy?
Probably,
Will be,
Eventually.
While I'm here
You disappear,
I'm depressed,
Can't rest,
I'm not surprised
Because through your eyes
She's far better than me.

Lucy Shaw (12)
Harton Academy, South Shields

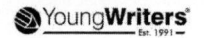

A Fat Cat

My cat is fat,
He always sits on his mat,
All he does is that.

Then I came one day,
And found out it died,
He always liked his food fried,
And then I found him in the kitchen,
He was fried alive.
Bye-bye
Fat cat.

Oliver Todd (13)
Harton Academy, South Shields

Lonely Man

Screams of the people,
As I stare through the peephole.
My life is all the same,
Everyone is scared of my name.
I wish they knew me,
But they all ran past me.

Millie Hall (13)
Harton Academy, South Shields

Buses

I am not a teacher, but you will learn from me,
I am not a car, but I get you where you need to be,
I am not a police officer, but will protect you like one,
I am always on a public service,
I always take photos when I'm at work,
I always am around Stamford, Bourne and Peterborough,
You see me in blue, creamy white, black colours,
When you get on you always hear a baby cry,
I'm always big or small,
I always travel on the road,
A vehicle that carries significantly more possessions than the average car.

Blake Fletcher (17)
Inspire Education Group, Stamford

War

Sitting in the dark, waiting for you,
All I can think about is you,
If you were here, the day would pass faster,
The faster time goes, the closer I feel to you,
I can't wait to see you again,
You mean the world to me,
And I am staying strong for you,
So please, just wait for me,
It won't be long, war is hard,
But I am doing it for you!

Brandon Jessop (17)
Inspire Education Group, Stamford

I Am Who I Am

I am not for everyone,
I know my truth,
I know who I am,
I know what I do and do not bring to the table,
I'm not saying I'm easy to deal with but I do bring tonnes of value,
I bring love and strength,
But I am not perfect.

Noah Smitheringale (17)
Inspire Education Group, Stamford

Drowned Out

A river of awkwardness,
Inconsistently flexible,
Shallow like a puddle,
But deeper than a murky pond,
Too shapeless to hold,
Yet, too leaky to retain,
Dripping with disaster,
I am lukewarm at best.

Shanna Larmond (17)
Inspire Education Group, Peterborough

Jojo Matters

Jojo's Bizarre Adventure, a sight to behold,
If you don't watch it, you'll start to mould.

The first season is terrible,
But the second is memorable.

Dio was, for sure, strong,
But he was definitely in the wrong.

Oops, spoilers, I'm sorry but it was too good, I couldn't resist,
With your mentality, it will for sure assist.

When watching it you'll float around in ecstasy,
It is a great made-up fantasy.

Please watch it, as it flatters,
Only because Jojo matters.

Lachlan Garside (12)
Kingsland School, Shaw

A Health Code Violation In Disguise

I am here to address a crime that is pineapple on pizza
You may think it's divine
But it's a guaranteed visit from Mr Reaper
Trust me, it's a crime
The most extensive form of torture
Poison in disguise
Not fit for your son or daughter
It's death before the eyes!
Now, some people say that fruit does not belong
What about tomato?
It's featured in many songs
Now we would like your opinion
Are we right or wrong?
Because pineapple is the colour of Minions
Does pineapple belong?

Lily Campbell (12)
Kingsland School, Shaw

Untitled

F ield
A griculture
R unning tractors
M uddy.

Josh Bell (12)
Kingsland School, Shaw

There Was A Life

Life seems to be longer than the river Nile,
If you swam through it, you'd swim for miles,
But by the river's steady flow,
Dreams may drift, triumph may grow.

Student life is not some breeze,
Heaps of homework, no social ease,
Activities beyond class for a successful theme,
Yet they tire you out like chasing a distant gleam.

"Your future is bright," they say,
Even though it's light-years away,
Yet it's opaque, full of amiss,
But within that obscurity, lies cosmic bliss.

Maria Wisniewska (12)
Longsands Academy, St Neots

Untitled

As I stroll through the woodland so grand,
Where nature's wonders await hand in hand.
The towering trees, majestic and tall,
Whisper secrets as autumn leaves gently fall.

A symphony of birdsong fills the air,
Their melodies weaving a tapestry rare.
The rustling of leaves beneath my feet,
Guides me along this tranquil retreat.

The scent of pine, fresh and crisp,
Invigorates my spirit with each gentle wisp.
Sunlight filters through the leafy canopy,
Painting patterns on the forest floor so freely.

I admire the intricate webs spun with care,
Silent artists creating masterpieces in the air.
Butterflies with vibrant wings outspread,
Flit and dance as if amongst dreams I tread.

Through the dappled shade, I continue my quest,
Discovering hidden gems, nature's very best.
A babbling brook, its waters crystal clear,
Whispers stories that only the forest can hear.

I pause by a clearing bathed in golden light,
Enchanted by its celestial sight.

A deer grazes peacefully, untouched by fear,
In harmony with surroundings so dear.

A symphony of silence, nature's gentle choir,
Transcends all worries, quelling my desire.
Here in the forest, lost yet so found,
Answers to questions softly echo around.

With a heart filled with wonder, I continue on,
Appreciating nature's rhythm, its tranquil song.
For in this forest, a journey to one's core,
A walk of solace and peace forevermore.

Phoebe Haynes (12) & Bella Farrier
Longsands Academy, St Neots

He Is

He is the body for my soul,
Now my body is gone.
He is the overpowering darkness that found me,
Without him I would be lost,
As I am now.
How I miss the moon's gaze,
Now I'm held captive by the overwhelming sun,
It feels like torture seeing his heart freeze.
I miss the cold winter nights
Where it was only his grasp keeping me warm.
Now I feel like I'm overheating,
This painful burning sensation
Is like being on the sun's surface.

He is the love of my life.

Georgia Jackson (13)
Longsands Academy, St Neots

She Was

She was
She was the soul for my body,
Now my soul is gone.
She was the overpowering light that kept me sane.
Now insanity consumes me.
How I long for the sun's comforting presence.
Now all I have is the moon's sickening stare.
I feel alone and distraught.
Was it the loss that started my demise
Or was it the cruel winter that froze me in the moment like her picture
That will forever sit on my mantle?
She was the love of my life.

Ruby Henson (12)
Longsands Academy, St Neots

A Pen Of Use

There I am, in the darkness
where I wait and wait
until when the light shines.
My owner only uses me a little
because all I am is a pen
with only a few days remaining.
Once my ink runs out,
what will happen?
Will I be trashed?
In the darkness forever?
Or what?
I wish I knew.
Now my time has ended.
I ran out of ink,
well, I hope I die
a painless death.
We will see.
I'm back in darkness, of course,
he really keeps all of his pens
that don't work
in his bag,
where others end up.
Now, I'm stuck here,
I guess I'm just as useless
as every other pen.

Alex Teicans (13)
Moor End Academy, Crosland Moor

Blitz Boy

From the whooshing of steam from trains
To children aboard, scruffy and well-dressed,
I boarded my train, peeking through the window,
Mother's smile hiding inconsolable glinting tears,
To the towering hills and mountains,
And the great stretched plains of grass.

A look at myself, checked with tag to say
To soul to take care of and suitcase
With my valuables.

Iremide Nasiru (13)
Moor End Academy, Crosland Moor

Dad's Gone

It's not nice being alone
With no father and no home
I think Dad may be dead
That's the only thing I dread

May have taken his life
But no, not with a knife
With the bullet through his heart
It reminds me of the start

The man in the trench
May die with the stench
They're probably gonna die
All there stood in a line
Never fell down in the line
Shoulder to shoulder this wasn't right

Children will cry
Not everyone will understand why
Taken away
Gone in a haze

Never seen again
From war nothing to gain
A war to be won
All the guilt from what they have done

Dad's not returned
6 years of hurt
And nothing ever worked

I visit his grave
No profile and no name
Wish he would have stayed
But now he's been weighed
On a scale of Heaven and Hell
His death on which I dwell

Still no home
Still all alone
It doesn't bother me
Living in pity
Making money off the streets
Not like a conner or a crook
But in a way that leaves people shook

You're reading this now
You're reading my work
My horrible experience
Did it leave you hanging off a hook?

Olivia Wright (11)
Ossett Academy & 6th Form College, Ossett

War Is No Game

I'm writing this to you, my boy,
Don't play with guns, not even a toy.
I've seen something of men, and bombs whistle,
And whirl.

The trench is cramped, damp and cold,
Young men arrive who never grow old.
The sky is filled with crimson tears,
Of bloodied men who face their fears.

I'm fighting people for who knows why,
My friends are dying, I want to cry.
So remember this, my cherished boy,
Don't play with guns, not even a toy.

Amber Barclay
Ossett Academy & 6th Form College, Ossett

Fading

I see into your eyes
They debunk your lies

You cover your frown
While cascading down

Leg bouncing, heart pounding
While your 'self' is fading

Feeling like you'll die
But still, you won't cry

It hurts to watch your blue eyes fade to grey
As you fade away.

Louie Nero (17)
Ossett Academy & 6th Form College, Ossett

Fire

My eyes open, the daylight seeps in,
A scene is before me, I cannot begin,
To describe the horror I see before me,
Doors reduced to blackened matchwood,
Rubble strewn across the mud,
Trees are vanquished, bent and broken,
Flowers shrunken, wilting, sad,
Stripped of their beauty by the forces of bad,
My mind is numb, my muscles ache,
And then I remember.

Blisters on my feet, bleeding raw,
A metal bird up high does soar,
And then, with an almighty cry,
I see fire raining from the sky,
The metal birds are gathering in flocks,
Hailing down their deadly shots,
Then I hear a loud, sharp sound,
Pain explodes in my head,
When I feel it for blood, my fingers come back red,
Screams echo louder, wood crashes down,
I totter to my cottage, or what is left,
Pick up the lifeless body of our cat,
And then the pain takes over.

I take one last look at the gold-and-pink sky,
I'll join them, it's time to fly.

Lucy Aditi Long (11)
Outwood Academy Bydales, Marske-By-The-Sea

The Last Elephant

Do you ever have that knowing feeling that something's going to go wrong?
That urge to run and hide from that eerie pong?
Well, that feeling and all the emotions that come with it swallowed me up and spat me straight out into a dark, bottomless pit.
I stood there, helpless like a lion that could not roar
or a dog with a pegleg instead of a paw.
And, as if my mind spoke the truth,
a crowd of humans led by a tall man with a golden tooth stormed through the jungle and out toward my family.
It was a rampage. It was a tragedy.
But, most of all, it was a huge group of sneaky, unreliable and crazy
serial killers. Blood spurted everywhere,
there were bones and organs and ripped-out hair.
There were screams and cries and roaring fire, but I just stood there, helpless like a mouse that could not speak or a lavish ceiling that had a leak.
But a bad sort of light flooded out
the top of my head, so, for a minute, I felt I stuck out like a knob on a tree.
So, I shone and I shone and I shone,
shone, shone, shone, shone.
"Hey," shouted someone from behind a bush. "I think we missed one...!"

Lenni O'Donnell (11)
Priestnall School, Heaton Mersey

Their Prayers

I look down below
to see this human race sink so low
the words 'kindness over cruelty' spoken no more
so I stay in the clouds of Heaven, stunned, in awe.
In awe of the people I refuse to protect
because when awe turns to horror, it's an ugly sight
everyone built from heart, brain and endless love.
And yet where is it now? Torn apart.
Killed, rebuilt, reborn.
Now with heads empty and hearts of stone
your heart rots away and the Earth does the same.

And they prayed. Let them pray.

Another century goes by, time really does fly
but the people don't change, like you were expecting them to?
So now, instead of empty heads and hearts of stone
all have screens for brains and nothing to show for heart
but you'll definitely see some 'hearts' around
just as long as it's filmed for all to see.
For all to see. For all the praise.

So they prayed. They prayed.

Pray for fame, pray for fortune
but it's never gonna come if you never try.

Pray for luck, pray for something, anything to change
but nothing will change if you do not.

For I am only an angel, I am no goddess
I may only guide, not live your lives.
And if that makes me unworthy, then so be it!
Take my wings and take my song.
And let us watch this doomed race fall into an abyss of despair
watch them all fall, my dearest, my love.
Let them pray.

Maryanne Ratanamook (14)
Priestnall School, Heaton Mersey

Through Their Eyes

Through their eyes, I glimpse the world anew,
A kaleidoscope of colours, vibrant and true.
In each gaze, a story unfolds.

Through their eyes, I see the pain,
Etched in lines, like a weathered terrain.
The weight they carry, burdens untold,
In silent battles fought, yet never bold.

Through their eyes, I witness the joy,
Like sunlit rays, no darkness can destroy.
In laughter and smiles, life's sweetest tune.

Through their eyes, I feel the love,
A gentle caress, like a soaring dove.
The warmth that blossoms deep within,
A connection so pure, it knows no sin.

Through their eyes, I taste the fear,
Like bitter tears that flow crystal-clear.
The trembling whispers, a heart's lament,
In shadows of doubt, they're never content.

Through their eyes, I hear the song,
A symphony of dreams, fragile and strong.
The melodies that dance upon their lips,
Unveiling secrets with each tender script.

Through their eyes, I learn to see,
The vastness of human complexity.
In every glance, a universe unfolds,
A spectrum of stories waiting to be told.

Through their eyes, I find my own,
A reflection of souls, intricately sewn.
For when we truly open our hearts wide,
We see the world's beauty through their eyes.

Billy Mcasey (16)
Priestnall School, Heaton Mersey

Hope

It's a shame how fast we come and go,
I say grab life by the horns! But 'take it slow'.
With nothing to live for, it's just a cycle with no end.
But you can decide to make amends,
To have a motive, a light that keeps you going.
Something that pushes you without even knowing,
When everything feels lost and gone,
Suddenly, all the lights are turned on.
Then you're happy, fearless, excited for what the future holds,
Everything slowly starts to unfold.
No one can change this,
Nothing can break this.
And I know this,
But the world doesn't wait,
You can't even say, "No!" Too late!
You try, but the world has no feeling,
And so the cycle again begins.
And I write again and again,
To find a joy is to find a dream,
To find a dream is to find a gleam,
To find a gleam is to find love.
People say it's only what you hope for,
Hope is to believe in what is invisible,
To say that is inevitable.
But through all the sorrow and sadness,

That hope starts to fade and so does happiness.
As all your pieces ebb away,
You lose faith and are led astray.
If only we didn't lose our hope,
Maybe it would have helped us cope,
If only we didn't lose our hope.

Claire Latunji (13)
Priestnall School, Heaton Mersey

Dysphoria

Sat alone in my room
Overwhelmed by endless gloom
Tears well up in my eyes
I thought I'd be happy, not telling lies

Stuck in a body I can't love
This wasn't the future I dreamed of
I change my look, I change my name
But the world still sees me the same

Everyone tells me that I'm broken
Even those closest to me left me heartbroken
Removing my binder feels more like removing my heart
Sculpting my face as if it's art

Eating alone every lunch
People hurl my deadname like a punch
Going outside feels like purgatory
The tears make the world go blurry

Hidden behind a tree, lacking all joy
Desperately repeating, "I am a real boy!"
Suddenly, a hand reaches out to me
Someone, a part of my community

Someone who relates to how I feel
A way to help us both heal

Because when your world feels like it's coming to an end
We have each other to help us mend

Talking may not cure dysphoria or fear
But it's a good reminder people are here
And even when the world is turned against us
We will remind them we are not to be left in the dust.

Edie Gravestock (13)
Priestnall School, Heaton Mersey

Silent Battles

I look up at the stunning sky,
The comforting, brilliant moon up high,
Somewhere, a shooting star passes by,
So many mysteries,
Beckoning us into the great unknown.

I look down into the deep blue sea,
And wonder what creatures there may be,
So many monsters and wonders waiting to be found,
Toiling in the darkness without a sound,
Until they eventually get dragged into the light.

I look into my chaotic mind,
So much noise you are yet to find,
But peel back the layers and you will see
Yourself into unfamiliar territory,
Soft stars in a forgiving sky,
Kind, gentle, calm and welcoming,
But you will discover the stars are fighting,
The rushing water down below,
Carving concave scars into jagged cliffs,
Alluring you into deep, dangerous rifts,
They fight for dominance, control.

How can you say you know the stars
When you have only gazed upon them from Earth?
How can you say you know the sea

When you have never dived into the depths?
How can you say you know me
When you have never looked past the calm surface?

Amelie Murray (14)
Priestnall School, Heaton Mersey

Times That Were

Behind the make-up and painted eyes,
There's a girl who every night cries and cries.
She decorates her body to trick the world,
But behind the facade, she's still just a little girl.

They say she is perfect, prim and proper,
But inside, she is a mess of melted copper.
They say she is wanted and needed,
But ignored her when she pleaded and pleaded.

On the inside, she is broken and crushed,
But each time she tries to speak, she just gets shushed and shushed.
Nobody cares about her or how she's feeling,
But if they knew the truth, their minds would be reeling.

She's no longer the happy, innocent girl they once knew,
But when they asked, she'd not reply and instead respond with a "How are you?"
The silence was eating away at her,
But now she can't go back to times that were.
She can't go back to times that were.

Charlotte Hill (12)
Priestnall School, Heaton Mersey

Teddy Bear

I am the bear you got in the hospital
That very day you were born
You lay beside me quietly
And let out a sleepy yawn

I am the bear who held your hand
And went with you to school on your first day
But I was only allowed to sit on the side
As you made friends and went off to play

I am the bear that saw you graduate
As you stood there in your hat and gown
With people cheering excitedly
As if you were wearing a crown

I am the bear that watched you at your wedding
Heart filled with pride
Though you talk to me less now
Our friendship has never died

I am the bear that helped you in your life
And was there for you in your highs and lows
I have now completed my duty
To watch and be there as my child grows.

Bethan Griffiths (14)
Priestnall School, Heaton Mersey

The Moonlit Realms Of A Poet

In moonlit realms where stardust weaves
a tapestry of dreams, the heart believes.
Whispers of the night, secrets untold,
in the symphony of verses, a masterpiece unfolds.
Beneath the canopy of celestial hue,
echoes of a poet's soul ring true.
Metaphors like comets streak the sky,
unveiling emotions that soar and fly.
In the garden of language, blooms desire,
each syllable, a flame, a poetic fire.
A sonnet of hope, a ballad of grace,
a lyrical journey through time and space.
Embrace the symphony, let feelings swell,
with the power of words, let the soul compel.
Through the valleys of metaphor and peaks of rhyme,
forge a poem that transcends the bounds of time.

Evan Dawson-Jones (13)
Priestnall School, Heaton Mersey

Anti-Social

Social media, a digital stage,
Where we share our lives and people engage.
Where our stress is held back by a blanket, all hidden away,
Like we have travelled to a different planet, longing to stay.

Scrolling through endless feeds,
Our eyes glued to the bright blue screens.
Comparing ourselves, planting its harsh, toxic seeds,
A break is what everyone needs.
But how do we pull away when we are tied up with leads?

How do we teens quit our lives on social media?
If only we were children again, that would make it so much easier.

Lola Broady (14)
Priestnall School, Heaton Mersey

A Blind Man's Sight

How much should we be obliged to know prior to confession?
Where should we stand?
And when should we stand up and be counted as equals?

Drowsiness, hours of night,
On a planet that is not right,
Humanity escaping liquidation,
A sort of nightmare that won't go away.

Individuals pummeling behind blue eyes,
Not hearing what they hear,
Not seeing what they see.

How far can they hold the rope until it starts to shred to smithereens?
How long should their heart be able to beat before it stops?

Laibah Nasir (14)
Priestnall School, Heaton Mersey

Blind

In my eyes, I see nothing,
I feel, smell, hear,
But yet I see nothing,

It would be nice to see the flowers grow,
The ones I love,
And the winter snow,

It would be nice not to have to rely on people,
But I know that means they care,
It would be nice to see my friends,
And to not feel so unaware,

In my eyes, I see nothing,
I feel, smell, hear,
But the only thing I can do better than anyone else
Is to not judge someone by how they look or appear.

Esme Maiden
Priestnall School, Heaton Mersey

A Time Of Crisis

It was fine until the war,
Which made everyone poor.
Then the explosives hit,
Which broke my heart just a bit.
My mother died from the bomb,
Like most people where I came from.
This war ruined my life,
Because my dad got stabbed with a knife.
All the troops tried to fight,
But at the end of the tunnel, there was no light.
I live in a different country now,
Sometimes, I ask myself how.
I was one of the few to survive,
Sometimes, I wonder how I'm alive.

Matthew Dansey (13)
Priestnall School, Heaton Mersey

Through The Eyes Of A Firefighter

999, an emergency call,
Courage, commitment, saving lives,
Anticipation of what it will be,
A burning building or a cat up a tree,
A flash of blue, an eruption of red,
Engulfing the burning building ahead,
Move swift, no haste,
Time to begin the chase,
A ferocious inferno up ahead,
An explosion of waves to stop the spread,
Move smart, move fast,
Our work is done at last!

Amelia Lyons (12)
Priestnall School, Heaton Mersey

I'm Just A Kid

I am just a kid,
But my dream is to have an education,
Yet I wish for a reunion,
I am just a kid,
What do you want me to do?
My job is to queue,
I am just a kid,
But I don't know the meaning of free,
I'm Palestinian.

Jude Al-Azzawi (11)
Priestnall School, Heaton Mersey

I'm Thankful For My Son

I'm thankful for my son, my ultimate pride and joy.
He gets me through hard times, sad times and more.
When I'm happy he makes me happier, he's undeniably perfect.
He's the only one that I would die for.

I'm thankful for my son, even when he is stubborn.
When he throws a fit, I try to keep him calm.
Or when he is crying, hopeless and feels forgotten.
We will comfort him any time he feels numb.

I'm thankful for my son, from now until forever.
I feed him all the knowledge, from his first word to his last step.
I teach him how to read, how to write and how to cook.
I watch him spread his wings, that's something I have to accept.

I'm thankful for my son, he's gotten older now.
I hope I've taught him everything I needed to.
And one day, I hope he'll run back to me with open arms.
Saying, "I really hope that you know I love you."

David Annuschat (13)
Rutlish School, Merton

I'm Doing Well

Dazed, as I strugglingly opened my eyes,
Papers piled up, exams partially revised,
What was once familiar, felt so unfamiliar,
And when they ask, "Are you okay?"

"I'm doing well," was all I said.

Disinterested, as I sluggishly sat in the corner,
Students enjoying themselves, contradicted with my shadow.
Papers piled up, endlessly, filled with crosses,
And when they ask, "Are you okay?"

"I'm doing well," was all I said.

Hopelessness, apprehensiveness, pensiveness,
Masqueraded behind my smile.
Tears, guilt, scars,
Masqueraded behind my smile...

"I'm doing well."

Jerry Li (15)
Rutlish School, Merton

From The Beach To The Colosseum

It is on days like this
That your laugh echoes with me the loudest
Where my skin craves for your touch
And my ears ring for your laugh

Aimless and alone
I drift through the places
We once claimed as our own

From the beach to the Colosseum
The alleyways to the museum
I advance from place to place
Grasping onto your fading traces

For some wounds would never fully heal
Even with the gruelling passage of time.

Echo Tai (14)
Rutlish School, Merton

Untitled

I swing from vine to vine
When something catches my eye

Falling trees which is a little unusual
As it continues, I realise I'm in trouble
Desperately trying to warn everyone
Out comes the hot, bright sun

Gasp! What have I just witnessed with my own eyes?
Then quietly I start to cry
My home is no longer
Time to get revenge and start this war.

Matthew Gardiner (12)
Rutlish School, Merton

Dupont

Ball magician
French leader
Constant fighter
Try scorer
Toulouse legend
Match winner
Constant tackler

I am Dupont.

Orlando Hales (11)
Rutlish School, Merton

The Good Old Times

As I sit here, reflecting on my life,
I think about the good old times,
when kids would play in the park
and watch the sun 'til dark.
Rushing home from school each day,
looking forward to going outside to play.
Every weekend, I would go out and about
with my family, without a doubt,
we would walk and talk for hours on end!
I always enjoyed our evening family meal
around the dinner table,
laughing and joking, discussing our day,
followed by hot chocolate and family games,
which became our tradition every day.

Daily link-ups with friends have now become
a call to them on FaceTime,
I miss those outdoor evenings and family games.
Only good memories of this time remains.
Now my time with friends is spent playing Roblox online,
I can spend hours in a gaming room
and not realising the lack of outdoor activities and exercise
can ultimately lead to our doom!

Weekends that were spent in the town
shopping with family and friends,
are now spent shopping online

and checking out the latest TikTok trends!
Those cosy evenings spent playing games
and chatting to our family,
are now a room full of people
all sitting on their mobile phones
and gadgets uncunningly.

As I sit here, reflecting on my life,
I think about the good old times...

Elizah Rehman (11)
St Thomas More Catholic Academy, Longton

A Creature Of Regret

I am not a man.

I am but a creature,
A wild animal.
The sinful acts I always sought
Had never made me full.

I always wanted revenge
For vengeance was my friend,
But I met the consequences
And my life came to an end.

The officers imprisoned me
And I knew then and there
That I would soon die at their hands
And it would surely be fair.

Sure enough, they told me that
The last half-hour of my life
Was upon me, and this news
Struck me like a sharp knife.

I knew that it was fully deserved
Yet I still sobbed, cried, wept.
I would speak for the last time,
And for the last time I was fed.

It was nearly time for my death,
And I chose the electric chair.
As I looked around I realised
That my situation wasn't rare.

I writhed in pain as I sat down
And my soul slowly descended.
I saw the Grim Reaper and knew
My life had officially ended.

And so I slave away in Hell
With Satan as my guard.
I'm trapped for eternity
And eat nothing but lard.

What have I become?

Wiktor Surgiel (11)
St Thomas More Catholic Academy, Longton

Through The Eyes

I wonder why the sky is blue
And why the grass is green.
Now I feel so very blue
As the sunset feels so free.
It's dark now and I can't see.
I'm home now, and not busy
I'm so tired and I'm freezing
Mom looking through the keyhole, peeping
She let me in and hugged me
As we started weeping

It's morning, now I'm warm
Outside I see my bike,
I see my parents preparing for a hike
Right now I'm not tired
Then I see my dad who just got fired
I'm so happy I got some sleep
Because I really really needed it.

Anyiam Victory (12)
St Thomas More Catholic Academy, Longton

What We Don't See

These humans think they have seen pain
It's only them being soaked by rain
Think about your mother's death
These humans must be deaf
They think they've seen enough since birth
But they haven't seen the hell on Earth
My home melting was the first
But my mother's death was the worst
I hate being a polar cub
I just need help, if only I could
As I float to the west
It's time to close my eyes and rest
If only you could know
That this is what they don't show
If only you could help me
But this is what we don't see.

Samuel Adams (11)
St Thomas More Catholic Academy, Longton

The Moon On My Wings

Dusk is near, our gaggle rises,
Together we ascend.
The picture of unity.
I am the needle
The leader of our skein.
We weave in and out of the clouds
Stitching perfect rows in the lilac sky.
Our V silhouette
Illuminated by the moon.
Honks of encouragement
Disturbing the setting of the sun.
Any doubts dispelled by the force of the tailwind.
We head south,
Towards windswept Wales:
The patchwork countryside
Muted by the sea.
We are the envy of the sky-
Commanding attention
As we retrace our route from the previous year.

Phoebe Beasley (12)
St Thomas More Catholic Academy, Longton

Beneath The Race Is A Heart

Beneath our race is our heart,
Does our colour go? No!
Till death do we part,
We pace the floor to and fro,
Thinking about how to make it go,
It's not fair, for when we go out we dread,
Covering our skin with a piece of thread,
For how long have we done this?
I can't believe we've done this,
For years, decades,
All of our aids,
They are just ignored,
But theirs unignored,
For the colour they are, they are adored,
The hate towards us and they are adored,
But beneath our race is our heart,
And till death do we part.

Sumiya Iqbal (12)
St Thomas More Catholic Academy, Longton

Through The Eyes Of A Cloud

I am a cloud, I am fluffy and soft
I cause the weather and cause the frost
Drip, drip, here comes the rain
And later it will come back up again
You can't see me when there's sun
Which gives you a chance to have some fun
I make the thunder, rain and snow
I have many purposes which you already know
I evaporate the water which I produce
And I hold it up and soon let it loose
The lightning goes *crack, crack*
Don't get struck, it's a painful attack
I'll see you soon my dear friend
And off I go to the end.

Megan Carnwell (11)
St Thomas More Catholic Academy, Longton

The Lives Of Bullies

I am a victim of bullying
Hurrying through the corridor
Whilst being chased down
School days are always terror
When he's around
People say he's a pain in the neck
But deep down I know he's a good person
There might be a lot of things
Happening at home
Abusive parents
Non-supportive siblings
So when you see a bully
Always remember
They are hurt too
So if you see them
Just give them a hug
They are people too
Hurt people.

Sochima Anaenugwu (11)
St Thomas More Catholic Academy, Longton

Being Free...

As I solemnly gaze at the fog,
The mist unveils and leaves me in shock,
A glorious river and fish, I can see,
My face is so gleeful,
Like hooray to me,

I wander down slowly,
Careful not to slip,
Well, perhaps it's abandoned?
Or maybe just it...

Suddenly, I notice houses of people,
Singing and dancing,
Happy and cheerful,
And I know this is where I'll be laughing,
Forever and safe,
And no one is falling.

Zozan Sulieman (12)
St Thomas More Catholic Academy, Longton

Ocean

I am the ocean
Bright and blue
I look at the golden surface
And I see you.

You standing there
Taking in the heat
Enjoying digging
The sand on your feet.

I rise and fall
Feeling happy and warm
You laugh and smile
As the sun rises a new day is born.

Khadija Sonko (11)
St Thomas More Catholic Academy, Longton

Through Her Eyes - Taylor Swift

Through her eyes,
Cornelia Street lies.
Screaming for her return,
But it's just another picture to burn.

Through her eyes,
She's dancing with her hands tied.
Footsteps echo as she enchants the crowd,
Flicking her jewels wherever allowed.

Through her eyes,
As the phone cries,
"The old Taylor can't come
To the phone right now, why? Cause she's dead,"
And everyone sees red.

Through her eyes,
As she does arise,
All the stars aligned,
And the crowd cries,
"You are a mastermind!"

Through her eyes,
She sees our lives,
And sings for those who cannot speak,
With her melodies sweet,
A language so unique.

Through her eyes,
A world of stories unfolds,
A Swift melody, a tale to be told,
Fearless, she stands in the spotlight, bold.

Through her eyes,
The archer takes aim,
A songbird in flight, not seeking game,
Style and substance, not just a name.

Through her eyes,
All too well recalls,
The highs and lows, the rises and falls,
Long live the memories within her walls.

Through her eyes,
A daylight after the storm,
With treacherous steps, emotions take form,
A kaleidoscope of colours, a vibrant swarm.

Through her eyes,
In the rhythm of life, she finds her height.
Guided by stars, her shimmering light,
Wildest dreams take flight.

Through our eyes,
She's an enchanting tale,
A constellation of stardust, a celestial trail.
Where emotions set sail,
Taylor Swift, in our hearts, will always prevail.

Asmithaa Arvind (13)
Sutton High School, Sutton

The Crow

A glossy sheen engulfs the verdant flora,
Snow glistens in the sunlight,
Like frozen stardust with a mythical aura,
But this pristine paradise has something to hide...
A truth that escapes all of the lies...
A crow roams this desolate land,
Evading all of its brutal command.

It treads obliviously on this place scored with war,
Something that time could never restore,
In a flurry of wind,
It takes to the wing...
Soaring and gliding,
Alongside with its kin,
It gazes down on the ivory snow,
Poppies standing upright like soldiers once slain.

The memories of the deceased,
Shroud this humble crow,
A tragedy that we could never hope to know.
The crow finally turns away to the east,
Above all else, it yearns for peace...

Alex Cummins (14)
Sutton High School, Sutton

Through Their Eyes

Mirrors reflect my shattered soul,
Reveals the heavy weight on my shoulders,
A burden that carries my secrets,
The myriad of flaws etched into my heart,
Awkward smiles, inner demons unfold,
Whispering tales of the monsters inside.

A spiderweb of insecurity knotted within,
Afraid it will crack, let the emotions leak through,
Afraid of what others will think, what they'll say,
Crackling cauldrons of voices bubble around,
"What is she wearing?"
"Ew, gross!"
"Still pink... really."

Fellow teenage lives could begin to thrive,
If not suppressed by judgemental eyes,
Piercing our confidence yet again,
One says, "Grow up."
"You're being childish."
Whilst others offer their contradictory view,
"That's too much makeup," they say,
"Stay young."

Unrealistic expectations echo and scream,
A storm brewing in my head,

Twisting and churning and aching with pain,
The world keeps on spinning,
Where to begin?

Florence Edwards
Sutton High School, Sutton

A Desire To Be Perfect

You wake up every morning looking up at the ceiling,
Looking for an answer, some sort of response,
Something to tell you why you are this way,
But you know anything you hear will be your imagination.

The way the stars align perfectly, even though they're in the dark,
Girls at school who look like models,
Dolphins dancing in the deep ocean,
The way blossoms bloom in the spring,
You look for a way, a reason to become perfect, perfect like these things.

Why am I like this way?
Thoughts that overwhelm you taking over your mind,
You look in the mirror, not recognising the person you've become,
The way you scroll through your feed endlessly,
Looking for an answer, some sort of reason why.

The sweet taste of sugar on your tongue,
The tan you get on holiday after lying beside the pool,
The fresh morning breeze on your skin,
The feeling of hair, after you wash it.

You want a better body,
You want better skin,
You want to be perfect,
Perfect, like these things you see.

Ruby Griffin (13)
Sutton High School, Sutton

Influencer

In a digital realm where followers flock,
An influencer's life, through their lens we unlock,
Capturing moments, sharing their style,
Their impact stretches across every mile,
With every post, they shape the trends new,
Their voice resonates, reaching me and you,
From fashion to beauty, they lead the way,
Inspiring millions day after day.

They craft their image, curated and fine,
Building a brand, one part at a time,
Through likes and comments they connect,
Creating a community, a bond that's perfect.

Deleena Ramful
Sutton High School, Sutton

Through Their Eyes

Life as a teenager,
May sometimes be hard,
So many obstacles,
Keep up your guard,
Not sure who's your friend,
Or if you're following the latest trend.

Though life as a teenager is cool,
You share your thoughts with others at school,
Similar minds you'll find,
Be true to yourself and kind.

Though life as a teenager is cool,
There's more pressure than ever,
To do even better,
Than the last year,
And be more clever.

Elmeirah Inchaud
Sutton High School, Sutton

Through Their Eyes!

In a world that tries to define,
They rise above, their spirits shine,
They challenge norms,
They break free,
A showcase of hope for all to see.

Their voices echo loud and clear,
Demanding equality year after year,
In their struggles, resilience lies,
Through their eyes, we empathise.

Let's stand together, hand in hand,
Supporting each other to make a stand,
For in their journey, we find our own,
Through their eyes, a world unknown.

Hannah Morley
Sutton High School, Sutton

Through Their Eyes

I awake on the cold, cobbled floor,
Sunlight streaming through the bars,
Casting a shadow on my face,
My nose twitches,
My food: empty,
My water: bare,
Languishing in my dismal cell, I ponder my life choices.

Why am I here?
Is this the end?

My thoughts are interrupted by the familiar footsteps of my jailor,
A mask of a grin,
Painting her face,
She bends to me,
"Come on Lulu, walkies!"

Jenna Hunt (14)
Sutton High School, Sutton

Through Their Eyes

Like how the sun sets for dawn,
The lights in his eyes long gone,
Is it time for goodbye?
Or is it time to fly?

Revisiting the stars of his life,
Remembering the honeymoon with his wife,
Oh, what great times,
But the bell of the dead chimes.

With a smile, he greets whatever comes next,
Another journey travelled through their eyes.

Audrey Yiu
Sutton High School, Sutton

A Murder

As I opened my eyes,
The police arrived,
All I could see,
There was a hand lurking towards me.

All I could see was the smothering,
Of the night that should have made history,
As blood dripped from side to side,
I started to cry.

Then I remembered a story,
A tragic story,
A murder that goes inside my head even further.

My friend got taken away,
As it made my day,
A gloomy day,
As gloomy as can be.

I can never trust anyone again,
As my one true friendship,
Came to an end,
As I cried a sea, day and night.

All I could see, a murder,
All I could see, was my friend,
A murderer,
All was the end.

Freya Nicholas (12)
Teddington School, Teddington

Anne Frank

After the Nazis had invaded us in 1939,
Everyone was not fine.
I am determined but scared,
Like the rest of my family, for whom I cared.

Everyone screams and hides,
Without any of our guides.
Many had passed away,
With Nazis' guns shooting in either way.

We remained in a nice hiding place,
Where we could not be traced.
I had left my home with my darling cat,
That had never been naughty or fat.

Miep always gives us food,
In a doubtful mood.
We always thank her with all our hearts,
Before she departs.

I don't think of all miseries but of the beauty that still remains.
The beauty that I never know how much it contains.
Enjoy the time you are here,
I had told myself without any fear.

I had written a diary with all my love,
More than peace represented by a dove.
I was thankful that I still had family.
I hoped people would send money through their charities.

I could hear banging of guns with my ears.
I can imagine crying children flooded tears.
I want to stop the Nazis from killing Jews,
But I can't, for I need to stay out of view.

One day,
We were given away,
By an unknown person,
That's when life had already worsened.

We are taken by the Nazis' army,
I am ready to let them harm me,
They point their guns at my head,
Bang! Oh no. I think I would be dead.

Melanie Chan (11)
Teddington School, Teddington

Mr Beast

I remember when I first started
Aged merely at thirteen,
I had a person for help
But my subs today were unforeseen.

In 2015, I became more popular
And as my channel grew,
I hired four childhood friends
To be the first of my new crew.

Soon, I had a new idea
To count to one hundred thousand,
Soon, there were loads of views
And many more subs to my channel.

I quickly gained popularity
Doing many weird and whacky stunts,
Like staying underwater for 24 hours
Or watching paint dry for grunts.

In the summer of 2022, I reached 100 million subs
And I knew my channel would thrive,
And in late 2023, I surpassed 200 million
Which I reached whilst being buried alive.

My video, 'Would you fly to Paris for a baguette?'
Is my most-watched video of all time,
It reached 1 billion views in less than a month
With over 40 million likes as well.

Seren Seah (11)
Teddington School, Teddington

Flowers

I'm the flower,
Given to anyone,
That's me.

I'm the tulip given to the sick grandmother,
Bringing a smile to her careworn face,
That's me.

I'm the daisy,
Given to the best friend,
For chains of friendship,
That's me.

I'm the red rose,
Given to the boy's girl,
Every February,
That's me.

I'm the violet,
Given to the grave,
Bringing a shred of hope,
That's me.

I'm the forget-me-not,
Given to the group of friends,
Sealing their promises,
That's me.

I'm the white rose,
Given to the bride,
Thrown and caught with laughter,
That's me.

I'm the poinsettia,
Given to the altar,
By the girl on Christmas Day,
That's me.

I'm the flower,
Given to anyone,
That's me.

Evie Sweeney (13)
Teddington School, Teddington

My Stolen Spark

They took my spark,
They stole it, I know it,
I used to draw long after dark,
However, now I wonder, confused from the bench where I sit,
What happened to imagination?
What happened to my mind that was once filled with colour?
Or was it just the world that faded?

She gave me my spark,
But this time it was different,
I still sit in the park,
However, instead of a pencil, I use a pen,
On lined paper, I do not doodle or draw,
I write, write my life away,
Next to my candle where my spark once lay.

Alicia Dickens (13)
Teddington School, Teddington

In Another Life

A heart that aches, with dreams to fulfil,
A soul that yearns to roam, to conquer the thrill,
A spirit that cries, the pain from within,
To soar and explore is not a sin.
But heavy chains that bind,
And how far away this dream is to find.
For freedom is a desire that's deep inside,
A longing for liberty that will never subside.
And still, I dream of flying high,
Of soaring to the sky, from which I'll never cry.
In another life...

Ella Lau (13)
Teddington School, Teddington

Silence

They tell me I'm a monster,
I laugh and tell them no.
They tell me I'm a sinner,
I say I don't repent.
They tell me I am worthless,
I point out I'm worthy to die.
They tell me I'm emotionless,
I describe how I don't care.
They tell me I should die,
I state how they have planned to kill me.
They ask me my last words,
I remain silent.

Sarah Evans (13)
Teddington School, Teddington

Just Gotta Make It To Friday

Alarm bells blaring through our brains, we get out of bed,
When you're waking this early, sleep is just pretend,
Our teenage anthem repeating in our heads,
Just gotta make it to Friday, reach the weekend!

Our uniforms are nothing to the freezing cold,
Everyone wearing the same thing? Please say, "Psyche,"
"You're not allowed to wear that, do as you are told,"
Just gotta make it to Friday, wear what we like.

Break and lunch is the only time we see our friends,
Our classes are too noisy, distraction awaits,
Held captive in a classroom, when will this end?
Just gotta make it to Friday, go out with our mates.

Time spent with family instead spent with homework,
We are working like adults, but we're only teens,
Missing assignments, making us go berserk,
Just gotta make it to Friday, achieve our dreams.

Just made it to Friday, we've reached the weekend,
Bored out of our brains 'cause everything's complete,
At least at school there's something to attend,
Now it's Monday morning, the cycle will repeat.

Amy Hawkes (14)
The Chauncy School, Ware

Why Is Our World Like This?

In a world obsessed with looks, let's redefine the game.
Embrace the beauty within and let go of the shame.
For every curve and scar, tells a story that is unique.
For our bodies are a canvas, where self-love can speak.
Remember what's inside that truly shines,
confidence and kindness are the greatest of signs.
Stand tall, and embrace your flaws,
and let your spirit soar
for beauty lies in every shape, size and more.

In a digital world where words can sting,
cyberbullying takes its cruel swing.
But we won't let hate be our guiding star,
together we'll rise and show who we are.
With kindness as armour, we'll stand tall.
Spreading compassion, we'll conquer it all.
Supporting each other, lending a hand.
Creating a safe space where respect will expand.
Remember words have power, both good and bad.
Let's use them to uplift and make others glad.
Stand against cyberbullying, take a stand.
In a world where empathy reigns hand in hand.

In darkness when pain feels too much to bear,
know that you're not alone. I'll always be there.
Through struggles and battles, we'll find a way.
Together we'll heal, one step at a time, day by day.

Your scars tell a story of strength and survival!
But remember, love and compassion are vital.
Reach out for help, let your voice be heard.
In moments of darkness, find solace in words.
You deserve kindness, gentleness and care.
Embrace the love around you, it's always there.
"Remember, my friend, you're never alone,
I'm here to support you with a heart that's your own."

In hallways filled with whispers and sneers,
fear and blame weave tangled snares.
But let's rise above, and break free from the chains.
Empathy and compassion are there where understanding remains.
Fear can grip us, and make our hearts race.
But empathy and kindness can find their place.
Instead of pointing fingers, let's lend a hand.
Creating a safe haven where understanding expands.
Blame may cast shadows causing pain.
But together we'll rise as a united domain.
Let's foster a culture of support and care!
Where judgement fades and compassion is rare.
We have the power to change.
To create a school where love will be arranged.
Let's stand together strong and true.
Embracing empathy in everything we do.

In a world where kindness should reign,
bullying causes so much pain.
Words like arrows are sharp and cruel.
Leaving scars that are hard to heal.
But let's be that change we want to see.
Together we can set hearts free.
We'll stand up strong united and tall.
Spreading love for one and all.
Let's be the light that shines so bright,
standing against bullying with all our might.
A smile, a kind word, can make a difference
creating a world where love exists.
Remember you have the power
to make someone's day brighter hour by hour.
Together, let's build a world so kind,
where bullying is left far behind.

This poem may answer a few questions, but not all.
This leaves us to wonder, why are people so cruel?

Sophie-Ann Bilton (11)
The Chauncy School, Ware

Enjoy Your Youth

People say, enjoy your youth,
People don't understand the pressure.
People say, enjoy your youth,
People don't understand having to do better.
The feeling of needing to surpass peers,
Only gets you laughs and jeers.

Online, the words you say,
Impact other people's day.
Perfect bodies on Instagram,
You now have to lose ten kilograms.
People comment things like, 'fat',
Come on now, guys, what's up with that?
Plumes of smoke emerge from every corner,
It's okay, at least you fit in.
Another one's lungs collapse, I tried to warn her,
She's damaging her future kin.
So the next time someone says,
Enjoy your youth, I'll just smile.
As I'm drowning in denial.

Rosie Hooper (12)
The Chauncy School, Ware

Playground Love

I'm in love!
New and exciting, like a brand new toy you get for Christmas,
A sort of playground love.

It's only been a month, yet I've known her soul for a lifetime,
Her messages shine a ray through my otherwise dull phone,
Her voice breaks through the traumas and pain I have faced.

As I begin to cling to her messages,
All I want is her,
A sort of playground love.

We meet up,
She looks perfect, everything is perfect,
As I touch her hand, my whole body ignites,
We skip through the shopping centre like toddlers,
I think I'm in love!

We sit down on the itchy, faded red seats,
The smell of popcorn nostalgically fills the air,
As the lights go down, my mind goes dark.

I need her,
I need to feel every inch of her,
I need her to see my love for her.

I get up to get more junk,
I always crave what I shouldn't have,
As I find my way back to my seat,
I realise the opportunity sitting right in front of me.

I reach my hands over her chair,
I feel powerful as I break her forbidden barrier,
As her smile fades, my heart feels the burning power take over,
I do it again and again,
She's mine.
A sort of playground love.

We meet up again,
The world is locked down by Covid-19, yet my love for her is free,
We walk through the abandoned streets... it's just us,
As she talks, I notice myself focusing more on her lips,
I need to kiss her,
I need to have her.

As I grab her hips, I feel her retract,
I ignore her as the burning power takes over,
I feel the stab of heartbreak in my chest as she pushes me away,
It's not my fault.

How selfish,
I don't talk to her for two weeks, that'll teach her,

She drives me crazy,
A sort of playground love.

She ignores my suggestive messages,
She ignores my remarks,
I know she wants it, so I'll give her one more chance.

I cycle two hours just to see her,
The sun is setting, reflecting on the calm waters,
Everything is perfect,
As I lean in for what is her final chance,
My body stops as a shock of ice smashes against my body.

What is happening?
I feel the once peaceful flowing river picking me up,
Violating my body.

It thrashes me around,
It had no respect for my boundaries,
It didn't consider if I was comfortable,
All it wanted was me.

What kind of monster would do that to someone?

Bea Wilding (16)
The Chauncy School, Ware

The Depths

I'm in my zone,
All on my own,
With nothing more to hurt me,
I am all by myself,
In the depths of the sea,
Lots of different creatures
Waiting there for me.
Watching, listening,
But something is missing.

But something else lurks,
I am not alone,
In the depths of the sea,
Something is there for me,
There's something big,
Dark and treacherous,
It lurks in the shadows
Of the depths of the sea,
Waiting for its prey,
AKA me.

Ruby Dare (11)
The Chauncy School, Ware

No Heaven For Man

See the old man,
Solitary, on my rocking chair,
They have all left me there.
Miserable, sick, my lungs turned black,
Only now I realise I can't go back.

My cracked visage fades, once and for all,
But worry not; I am still here, I remain for the fall.
I sink into my chair, no comfort to attend me,
The old man perishes, for what man is he?

Something is wrong, very wrong.
I expected Heaven, perhaps Hell,
But the world carried on.
I am dead; my body rots!
But aware is my mind; dead I am not!

For days, I rest there,
Comfort to only those vermin
Who pick at my wrinkled flesh,
I do nothing but sit,
At least I am fresh.

Shakespeare, Wilde, Plato.
We are but equals in our silent misery.
All men are equal, all in death's embrace.
All bones are equal; all flesh is grass.

My neighbours smell me.
That face is sunken, my yellowed eyes blank.
It takes three days for them to free me.

They take my identity,
A tag of lies hanging from my toe.
I scream for help, for them to stop,
I am alive!
I am still alive!

They drain my blood; I feel every second of it.
I feel weary; still, my tortures continue.
My eyes are pressed shut with needles.
They call me 'It',
For I am no longer human.

The mortician slides me into the cold, metal dark,
But I do not fear; I am surrounded by friends!
Other souls in the tombs,
Doomed to identical fates.

After another week, they put me into the ground,
Oh, the wretched ground!
I stay there to this day.
My grave is unattended by my grandchildren,
They leave me there,
Not knowing I can still hear them.

I am still here.

Ashton Lee Read (15)
The Chauncy School, Ware

Emergency Landing

Warning, warning, the thruster systems go,
I brace in despair as I ricochet to and fro,
My shuttle bolts like a comet, piercing the air,
I plummet to this rock, blazing like a flare,
Gasping for breath, I beam down beneath,
It's a restless, wavy substance to my disbelief,
It has no colour, no true shape or form,
It has me befuddled into a deep brainstorm.

I wait for an impact, ready for a hard batter,
But as I land I hear a peculiar splatter,
I stare up and find this abnormally odd,
My view is disorientated from inside my pod,
I cannot comprehend this anymore,
I release the airlock and open the door,
Gallons of substance slosh in every direction,
I flee from it all and buoyancy starts my ascension.

I reach a coast filled with stony features,
Far in the distance, I see strange, new creatures,
Each step by step, I walk across the beach,
Each time the creature is just beyond reach,
I scale a cliff and call out to it, "Stay!"
But the creature in fright has already run away,
Instead, I play stealthy and follow it home,
Its habitat is a tall wall made of thick stone.

I examine a door and leap straight through,
The creature stands still as if it were stuck in glue,
Strands of silky string protrude from its head,
It stares at me without speech, as if it were dead,
Its smooth, veiny skin is covered in apparel,
This new figure is the one they call mammal!
It shrieks in terror and gapes into my eyes,
It runs, it trips, "Alien!" the man cries.

Isaac Man (11)
The Chauncy School, Ware

Imagine A Rock

Imagine a rock.
A metaphor worn by beak.
Mine, to be precise.
It was purposefully phrased,
So I'm the greatest clock.

But I must thank you!
You helped my ticking so much
As my mountain lies
Where all mountains lie in truth.
And you realised early, too.

Then you saw my job.
Unbelievable, really!
You gave me my birth.
You could've caged me, but no,
You sped up my lifespan's work.

You don't remember?
In the thousand years waited
You wore it near down.
I've watched you advance,
So I'll sharpen my beak.

On masses of coal,
On corpses and corporate pride
On the sky itself!

One day of eternity
The final day to go by.

Soon I shall strike it,
And everyone's days shall cease,
So I thank you all
For making it so easy
For twelve to ring forever.

Alex Munt (15)
The Chauncy School, Ware

The Passel In The Zoo

We are used,
Don't get us confused,
You're the possum,
You're the opposum,
I am not you,
I am pretty new,
You live in the Southern Hemisphere,
And I live in the northern atmosphere,
We are defensive,
Not aggressive,
We don't like to fight,
But if you try, you'd get a bite,
We are cute,
And we both love fruit.
I live in a tree,
Marshes is my key.

Malaqai Burgess (11)
The Chauncy School, Ware

When You Dare To Be Different

Some kids play football,
Others do nothing at all,
But we kids can't always be brilliant
Because we dare to be different.

We can do some impressive things.
Our unique personalities bring
Joy to everyone's lives
When we dare to be different and thrive.

We may not be the same,
But we don't mind,
Because we dare to be different.

Zac Hashmi (14)
The Chauncy School, Ware

The Ghost Town

G ently, the wind blew through the empty streets,
H urriedly, the civilians ran to their crooked homes,
O bliviously, the ghosts flew through the abandoned mansions,
S ilently, the scared town folk nervously ventured to the markets,
T errifyingly, the floors creaked and the street lights flickered,

T iming their escapes correctly, the people slipped into their gardens and locked their gates,
O minously, the ghosts taunted the pets in people's homes,
W arning the adults, the mayor travelled around town,
N ervously the families snuggled up together and prayed for themselves as I watched them through their windows, keeping them safe.

Rowan Turnbull (13)
Vale Of York Academy, Clifton Without

Piano Pelagic

Waves crashed hard against my window,
A blowing sea under velvet sky: ablaze.
A final lull for my head upon my pillow,
My mind hooked - anchored on your gaze.

A Coriolis of coral embers, a cyclone,
My thoughts hold no conviction here,
But this, from the piano I hear melodies groan,
The composition sweet and clear, I reminisce.

It's the keys that yearn for canvas,
And I ache to paint upon them,
The ocean, the distance between the notes, it grows,
All my banks break, flooding emotion.

Meet me where the air skims the sea,
Where my thoughts swirl and dissipate,
Take me in your arms and hold me,
Let me float, fly,
Hesitate.

Amanda Chittock (16)
Vale Of York Academy, Clifton Without

Me And Them

I am the prey the lion chased from the den,
The victim of war driven from their home.

Every laugh and every look sends me to that darkened place,
The one where insults and self-doubt slap my face,
Splash cold water on my trembling body until it trickles down my back,
Turning to a pool of every foul word said.

What's happening to them now?
Them, surrounded by smoke and bombs,
Me, surrounded by pointed fingers and hushed mockery.

Me, sat alone in a seat, in a puddle of my own self-doubt,
Them, at the only home I've ever known, sat in a puddle of blood from the ones they love.

Olivia McPherson (13)
Vale Of York Academy, Clifton Without

Untitled

Sport, you either love it or hate it,
You can watch it and play it,
But don't deny,
That it is divine.

Sport, you either love it or hate it,
Whether it's football or rugby, basketball or tennis,
You don't have to like it,
But you have to try it.

Sport, you either love it or hate it,
But there is one thing about it,
It is mighty, mighty fun.

Ignacio Lloyd-Moliner (12)
Vale Of York Academy, Clifton Without

The Light

Though it may be hard,
Though it may be blinding,
Follow the path,
The good person will find you,
The light may be blocked,
By unwanted hands,
Your emotions will guide you,
The good person will find you,
Your path is your own,
Your own to construct,
The good person,
Is right beside you.

Jamie Elsworth (13)
Vale Of York Academy, Clifton Without

Through The Eyes Of Taj Mahal

Thousands of people every day,
Each individual has their equal pay,
I feel great to see those happy faces,
Talking and walking at different paces.

My eyes sting through the burning sun of India,
They wear shady things, this makes them look peculiar.
They eat and talk all day long,
All I hear is *chomp chomp chomp*.

I get told I am a symbol of love,
I can see flying doves,
I feel ashamed of the mistakes I have made,
Each one on a different pay.

All of us individuals pay at different cost,
But soon in the winter my turrets will frost.
The richness of my beautiful shape,
Will soon eventually fade away.

Romeo Barrett (11)
Wellingborough School, Wellingborough

Through The Eyes Of An Old Teddy

Children come in to look at all the teddies,
But sadly, not at me.
They turn their nose up at my elderly look,
And quickly turn away.

I am not scary or mean,
I am simply different, you see.
No fresh, fluffy coat of fur,
No long whiskers curling around my cheeks.

My eyes are small, round and scratched,
My ears are long, thin and ruffled,
My nose stitched and a dirty pink,
My stuffing falling out.

I am not bad, just old,
Worn out on the outside,
But inside, I have a heart of gold,
Just waiting for someone to love.

You stop and look and smile,
Could it really be?
Is this the day my dreams come true?
Will you choose me?

You take my hand gently,
And show me to your mum,
"This warm and cosy teddy,
Is really the perfect one."

She takes me to my new home,
And perches me on her bed,
I sleep with her every night,
And plant dreams in her head.

Remember when you look
To see more than just the outside,
The most special part is always hidden,
But its love stretches far and wide.

Elise Pettican (11)
Wellingborough School, Wellingborough

Eyes Of A Rat

I walk, and I talk
All day long,
Though I get sad because I pong,
"Money, help me please," I beg,
I'm only a small rat,
"Help me," I say,
As I beg and I beg.

I'm cold and I'm wet,
As I shiver and quiver,
"Please help me," I beg,
Give me warmth,
Give me liver.

I'll snack on anything,
A cat or a dog,
Maybe a horse or even a boar,
Most deer are near,
But I still cry a tear.

My tail is long,
My face is small,
Please help me beg,
As I crawl and I crawl.

As time flies by,
Rain or sun,
As I cry and cry,
"Please help me, please," I beg,
I say, as I beg and I beg.

Hattie Scott (11)
Wellingborough School, Wellingborough

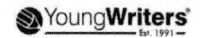

Through The Eyes Of A Flame

My life is full of heat and passion
But my life is short;
My life is fierce,
But always hot.

I can see the people who fear me
But all our lives end in ashes.
Their fears are as short as my life
But hopefully, they'll turn into happy fears
One day when I am gone.

I am the brightest light,
I am seen as elegant,
I heat people with my beauty.
This is my life.

My life is full of heat and passion
But my life is short;
My life is fierce
But always hot

One day I will die out
Someone will take my place
But this is the life I dream about.

Scarlett Howes (12)
Wellingborough School, Wellingborough

Through The Eyes Of A Poltergeist

In the dead of the night, when all is quiet,
An unseen creature is causing riot,
Tossing and throwing multiple things,
This ghostly monster has the living under its wing.

No one can see its unknown face,
Some might say it's of another race,
Yet it seems to attract attention,
Some might say it's redemption.

Scaring the residents out of their house,
Almost like a cat chasing a mouse,
But no one can escape this cat.

When the sun ascends high in the sky,
The poltergeist must say its goodbye.

Sam James
Wellingborough School, Wellingborough

Young Writers Est. 1991

YOUNG WRITERS INFORMATION

We hope you have enjoyed reading this book – and that you will continue to in the coming years.

If you're a young writer who enjoys reading and creative writing, or the parent of an enthusiastic poet or story writer, do visit our website **www.youngwriters.co.uk**. Here you will find free competitions, workshops and games, as well as recommended reads, a poetry glossary and our blog. There's lots to keep budding writers motivated to write!

If you would like to order further copies of this book, or any of our other titles, then please give us a call or order via your online account.

Young Writers
Remus House
Coltsfoot Drive
Peterborough
PE2 9BF
(01733) 890066
info@youngwriters.co.uk

Join in the conversation!
Tips, news, giveaways and much more!

YoungWritersUK   YoungWritersCW
youngwriterscw   youngwriterscw